Praise for
Helping Your Child Overcome Reading Challenges

"I love this book. I'm not a teacher by trade, and I had no clue about how to help my daughter with reading. Dr. Tracey provides suggested books and engaging activities that make learning fun."

—*Lisa K., parent*

"I read this book with great interest as both a parent and an educator, and came away inspired with ideas to help my own children and share with colleagues. Dr. Tracey takes us inside the life of developing readers and provides a positive roadmap for joining children on their literacy journey. The book offers stories of real kids and families alongside practical tools, resources, and easy-to-implement activities. A 'must read' for all parents who want to support the developing readers in their lives!"

—*Heather Kenyon Casey, PhD,*
Department of Teacher Education,
Rider University

"Dr. Tracey has written a winner! This is an essential guide for any parent whose child has difficulties with reading. It has a strong research and practical base, plentiful examples, and hands-on activities at the end of each chapter. For me, this book is the best on the market."

—*Patricia A. Edwards, PhD,*
Department of Teacher Education,
Michigan State University

Helping Your Child Overcome Reading Challenges

Also from Diane H. Tracey

Lenses on Reading, Third Edition: An Introduction to Theories and Models

Diane H. Tracey and Lesley Mandel Morrow

Helping Your Child Overcome Reading Challenges

Diane H. Tracey, EdD

THE GUILFORD PRESS
New York   London

Copyright © 2022 The Guilford Press
A Division of Guilford Publications, Inc.
370 Seventh Avenue, Suite 1200, New York, NY 10001
www.guilford.com

Printed in the United States of America

Last digit is print number: 9 8 7 6 5 4 3 2 1

Library of Congress Cataloging-in-Publication Data is available
from the publisher.

ISBN 978-1-4625-4380-9 (paperback) — ISBN 978-1-4625-4822-4 (hardcover)

The illustration of the parallel distributed processing model that
appears on page 6 and elsewhere in the book is from *Beginning to Read*
by Marilyn Jager Adams. Copyright © 1990 Massachusetts Institute of
Technology. Adapted by permission of The MIT Press.

The word family and sight-word lists in the Appendix are from *The
Reading Teacher's Book of Lists* by Jacqueline E. Kress and Edward B. Fry.
Copyright © 2015 John Wiley & Sons. Reprinted by permission through
the Copyright Clearance Center, Inc.

To my four grandchildren—
Benjamin Loizeaux Swain,
Linden Gerard Swain,
Redford Baldwin Swain,
and Baby #4 on the way—
may your lives be filled with light and love

Contents

Acknowledgments ix

Author's Note xi

1 Help! I'm Overwhelmed! 1

2 The Foundations of Reading 12

3 The Parts of the Reading Process 29

4 How Can I Tell What's Causing My Child's Reading Difficulty? 39

5 What Should I Do If My Child Is Having Difficulty with Visual Processing? 57

6 What Should I Do If My Child Is Having Difficulty with Auditory Processing? 71

7 What Should I Do If My Child Is Having Difficulty with Phonics? 87

8 What Should I Do If My Child Is Having Difficulty with Vocabulary? 104

9 What Should I Do If My Child Is Having   116
Difficulty with Reading Comprehension?

10 What Should I Do If My Child Is Having   131
Difficulty with Attention and/or Motivation?

A Few Final Words: Putting It All Together   145

Appendix: Word Family and Sight-Word Lists   153

Index   171

About the Author   178

Acknowledgments

I would like to begin by acknowledging the contributions of Chris Jennison, Craig Thomas, Kitty Moore, and Christine Benton, all of The Guilford Press, who have so skillfully and kindly guided and supported me as a Guilford author since I first started writing for them in 2001. Chris Jennison was my first editor and, following his retirement, placed me in the very capable hands of Craig Thomas. As my work changed from academic writing to writing for the general public, Craig guided me to editors Kitty Moore and Christine Benton. What a joyful collaboration this has been! From our very first conversation, there has been an extraordinary synergy among the three of us that might be unique to seasoned professional women joining forces. Sincere thanks, Kitty and Christine! I am deeply grateful for the exceptionally fine experience of having worked with you on this book.

I would also like to acknowledge the literacy and psychoanalytic professional communities at large. My first career as a literacy educator and professor for 25 years was deeply enhanced by my teachers, colleagues, and students from Rutgers University, Kean University, the Literacy Research Association, and the International Literacy Association. Of special note is my mentor and dear friend, Lesley Morrow, who provided me with ideas, encouragement, opportunities, and loyal friendship as I built my literacy career. My second career as a psychoanalyst has been profoundly shaped by my teachers, fellow students, and patients at the Center for Modern Psychoanalytic Studies in Greenwich Village, New York City, where I currently study and work. Here I want to particularly note the contributions of Sara Sheftel, who has helped me to achieve my dreams while providing me with a model of successful living.

I am also blessed to have a network of smart and fun-loving friends who enrich my life in every way. Nancy Wolf, you will always be my soul sister and BFF, and thank you for helping me write this book! William Storer, Heidi McCallum, Laura Otani, Robyn Rajs, Stephanie Solaris, Aleta LaBorie, Kathleen Conroy, and Maryanne Serafin, thank you for bringing laughter, good times, and support into my life. To Carol Malkin, thank you for being a great friend, for being the first outside reader of the manuscript, and for your thoughtful feedback on it.

My family is at the core of my being. To my daughters, Julia Tracey and Katherine Tracey, it is hard for me to express how much I love you and how proud I am of both of you. To Jake Shearer and Zachary Swain, thank you from the bottom of my heart for being such wonderful men, and such wonderful partners to Julia and Katie. To Benjamin Swain, Linden Swain, Redford Swain, and Baby #4 on the way, my grandchildren—wow! You light up my world, and I could not love you more. To my sister, confidante, and dear friend, Barbara Hirschmann, I'm so grateful that you're my lifelong companion for this journey. To David Elinson, thank you for your friendship, and for all the love, music, joy, laughter, and delicious food that you bring into our family. To Samantha Lewis, Luke Lewis, Hannah Lewis, Julius Elinson, and Paige Garratt, it gives me great joy to continue to deepen our relationships over the years. To Bunny Hirschmann, Chuck Dolan, Wayana Dolan, and Adina Hirschmann, I'm glad that our connections continue to grow. To my cousins, Ann Bikales, Norman Bikales, Phyllis Yarvis, and Richard Yarvis, the shared years make our conversations and visits all the more precious. Also, to my extended family on the Tracey side, thank you for your continued warm and loving embrace. In loving memory, thank you to Terry Hirschmann, Hank Hirschmann, and Betty Hirschmann. Last, but certainly not least, to the private man in my life, you have a most special place in my heart and soul.

Author's Note

In this book, I alternate between masculine and feminine pronouns when referring to a single individual. This choice has been made to promote ease of reading as our language continues to evolve and not out of disrespect toward readers who identify with other personal pronouns. I sincerely hope that all will feel included.

The parents who generously contributed helpful ideas in the quotations used throughout this book are identified with their permission. Likewise, teachers also generously offered tips for parents, and have been identified with their permission.

1

Help! I'm Overwhelmed!

> You gain strength, courage, and confidence by every
> experience in which you really stop to look fear in the
> face. . . . You must do the thing that you think you
> cannot do.
>
> —ELEANOR ROOSEVELT (overcame
> reading difficulty to become First
> Lady of the United States)

There are few things more upsetting to parents than watching their children struggle and not being able to help them. Some children struggle physically; they have difficulty overcoming an illness or injury or reaching age-appropriate, developmental milestones. Other children struggle emotionally and/or socially; they have trouble finding and/or maintaining their emotional equilibrium or developing friendships. Still other children struggle academically, with the basic tasks of learning seemingly harder for them than for their peers. In some cases, children struggle in all three realms. Almost always, parents want—perhaps more than anything in the world—to help their children, but they often just don't know how. As parents, we are typically not trained as physicians, therapists, or educators. As a result, we are at a loss to best help our children when they may need help the most.

Moreover, as parents we have our own struggles. We need to keep ourselves physically healthy and, as much as is reasonably possible, in a state of emotional stability (or at least sanity!). In addition, we almost always have relationship, work, financial, and social pressures. All of these demands occur in the context of an increasingly complex world in which the safety and well-being of our local, state, national, and international communities are at risk. No wonder we feel overwhelmed.

Now throw a child's reading difficulty into the mix:

Roger and Lauren are a professional couple with two children: Samuel (age 7) and Jasmine (age 5). Roger and Lauren both work long hours trying to provide their children with every life advantage. Despite their efforts, Samuel is having an unusually hard time learning to read. In kindergarten, he had trouble learning his letters and their associated sounds. In first grade, he couldn't master sight words. Now, in second grade, Samuel's teacher is talking about the possibility of getting him tested for a suspected reading disability. Roger and Lauren, already stressed by managing their own careers and family, are unsure of how to proceed. Will it be helpful to have Samuel tested and possibly given a "special education" diagnosis? What will happen if they proceed with the testing? What will happen if they don't? Is there anything that they can do at home to help?

Missy is a recently divorced mother of a young child, Michael (age 8). In addition to learning how to survive as a single parent, Missy is working full time. On top of this, Michael is struggling with his third-grade reading. He didn't seem to have any difficulty with his schoolwork before his parents' divorce, but now his academic performance is slipping, and his motivation to practice reading is low. Like many children his age, Michael only wants to play video games, spend time on his iPad, and watch television. How should Missy proceed? She's considering hiring a therapist or tutor, but her budget is tight, and professional services are expensive. Should she take away his screen time as punishment for poor school performance? Should she help him herself? If so, what can she do?

Binta and Jamal recently moved to the United States for Jamal's job. Although Binta and Jamal are excited to provide their daughter, Amira (age 12), with the international experience of living in the United States, they miss the warmth and support of having extended family nearby. In addition, both Binta and Amira have limited English proficiency. As a result, Binta is having trouble making friends in the community, and Amira is having difficulty in school. She spends part of her school day in a class for English language learners, but for the rest of the day she is in a regular seventh-grade classroom and is struggling with her schoolwork, especially with reading. It seems that Amira can pronounce the words in her books but doesn't know what all of them mean. Consequently, she can't understand what she is reading. What can Binta and Jamal do to help their daughter?

This book can help you strengthen your child's reading skills regardless of your child's age, grade, developmental stage, or diagnostic status. In this book I offer guidance about how you can help your child with reading problems, from understanding the reading process and getting a sense for what parts of the process your child is having difficulty with, to addressing those specific problems at home with a wealth of activities and resources I've compiled over many years. Of course, sometimes you'll also need professional help from your child's school, your pediatrician, or various specialists. You'll find more information about when to seek outside help in Chapter 4 and throughout the subsequent chapters. This book is about what *you* as a parent can do, regardless of whether your child has undergone testing or received a diagnosis. While this book is primarily written to meet the needs of parents of children with reading challenges, parents of all readers will likely find it helpful.

Understanding the Complex Nature of Reading Difficulties

As I think about the areas of strength and challenge demonstrated by families, I reflect on the many dimensions each of us has. In my worldview, each of us has physical, emotional/social, and cognitive dimensions. Many of us believe that we have a spiritual dimension as well. *As a result of these beliefs, over the course of my lifetime and training, I have come to the realization that the physical, emotional/social, and cognitive dimensions of each child must be considered to comprehensively understand, accurately diagnose, and effectively treat reading challenges.*

A number of personal experiences led to this insight. A very long time ago (about 30 years!) when I was a young mother, I came down with pneumonia. I had always previously taken my good health for granted, so I didn't think much of it when my original cold turned into bronchitis. The bronchitis didn't go away unfortunately and, even though I was following my doctor's advice, one day I realized that I couldn't walk across the room without getting weak. Something was definitely not right! At that point I was diagnosed with pneumonia.

The illness was a wake-up call for me, in that I started to understand the foundational importance of physical health in overall functioning. I ended up in bed for several weeks, and I couldn't enjoy or care for those I loved or for myself. I couldn't work. I was too tired to even read. I didn't feel like myself; I felt like a different person! Having pneumonia taught me that, when our physical functioning is compromised or less than optimal, all of our functioning (physical, emotional, and cognitive) is compromised. Recovering from pneumonia taught me about the critical importance of nutrition, sleep, and exercise in overall well-being. Specific to this book, my experience with pneumonia helped me to understand the relationship between a child's physical foundation, which is created by nutrition, sleep, and exercise, and a child's cognitive functioning.

I had a similar experience in the emotional realm. After the birth of my second daughter, I experienced a mild, but noticeable, postpartum depression. Similar to the time I had pneumonia, I just didn't feel like myself. I didn't want to, or couldn't, fully engage in all of my normal activities, or fully enjoy or care for those I loved or for myself, or work to my best ability. This experience helped me understand the central importance of my emotional health in my overall functioning and, in particular, the central importance of emotional health in general to cognitive functioning.

As my graduate studies deepened, I came across a third source of information that underscored the interdependent relationships of physical, emotional/social, and cognitive functioning: the famous work of Abraham Maslow (1943), known as Maslow's hierarchy of needs. In this theory of human motivation, Maslow proposed that humans have five levels of needs: physiological, safety, love and belonging, self-esteem, and self-actualization. Maslow hypothesized that one's physiological and safety needs had to be secure before one is motivated to focus on upper-level issues, such as love, belonging, self-esteem, and, ultimately, self-actualization. Maslow's hierarchy of needs, depicted in the diagram on the facing page, became an academic and theoretical affirmation of what I had personally experienced. Indeed, for every human being, cognitive

Maslow's Hierarchy of Needs

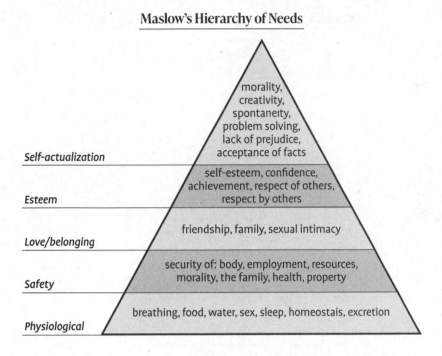

functioning (for example, reading ability) is built on a foundation of physical and emotional functioning.

A fourth piece of the complex nature of reading difficulty became clear to me as I was writing my first book, *Lenses on Reading: An Introduction to Theories and Models* (Tracey & Morrow, 2017). In that book I examined what is known as the parallel distributed processing model (PDPM; *Parallel Distributed Processing: Volume 1, Foundations,* Rumelhart & McClelland, 1986), shown in the diagram on the next page, as one of the best models available for articulating what happens during the reading process.

The PDPM conceptualizes reading as taking place in four interconnected processors in the brain: the orthographic processor, where the visual processing of print takes place; the phonological processor, where the auditory processing of sound takes place; the meaning processor, where vocabulary meanings are attached to identified words; and the context processor, where the construction, comprehension, and metacognitive

Modeling the Reading System: Four Processors

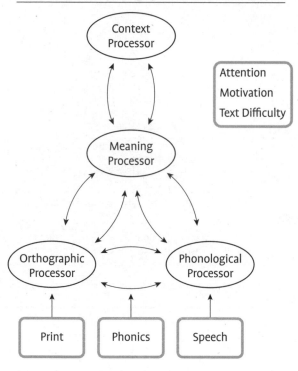

monitoring of the text message occurs. In addition, print and sounds are matched through phonics, which leads to word identification in the low-level processors of the model, and the entire model is organized according to the principles related to attention, motivation, and text difficulty. The PDPM provides a heuristic for understanding what needs to happen during reading for text comprehension to occur easily and efficiently. Moreover, as I fully explain in the following pages, the PDPM can be used as a diagnostic tool to identify weaknesses in a reader's specific processors, thereby illuminating paths for targeted, accurate, and effective intervention.

You don't have to be a reading specialist to benefit from this model or from an understanding of Maslow's hierarchy of needs, as this book is dedicated to helping you fully and accurately understand, monitor, and help your child in the areas highlighted by Maslow and identified in the PDPM.

What about Dyslexia?

According to The Yale Center for Dyslexia and Creativity, dyslexia is "an unexpected difficulty in reading in an individual who has the intelligence to be a much better reader." Using this definition, many children in the United States and around the world can be considered dyslexic. At the same time, there is often great disagreement about the use of the term and the criteria for its formal diagnosis. Moreover, while dyslexia is recognized as a disability by U.S. federal law, the Individuals with Disabilities Education Act, most U.S. school districts do not use this diagnosis as a basis for children's intervention and treatment. Given the controversy surrounding the term *dyslexia*, in this book I have chosen to use the general term *reading difficulty* instead. Please note that, whether or not your child has been diagnosed or might be diagnosed with dyslexia, the explanations of the reading process, of the sources of reading difficulty, and of the ideas for targeted reading interventions presented in this book are appropriate for your use. If, in addition to reading this book, you would like more specific information about dyslexia, the Yale dyslexia center and the book *Overcoming Dyslexia* (Shaywitz & Shaywitz, 2020) are excellent resources.

Who Am I?

Perhaps you are wondering why you should trust me or take my advice, so let me tell you a little about myself. Like many educators, I wanted to be a teacher for as long as I can remember. Growing up, I was the child who lined up all the other kids in the neighborhood and pretended to be their teacher. As I got older, I earned a teaching certificate and a bachelor's degree in psychology, taught briefly in the area of early childhood education, and then went back to school for a master's degree in educational administration and a doctoral degree in literacy education. In 1994, I began my career as a professor of literacy education at Kean University, one of the state universities in New Jersey. As a professor, I taught undergraduate students who were enrolled in teacher education courses how to teach reading to their future students. I also taught graduate students who were already teachers, and helped them become reading specialists—educators who specialize in helping students with reading difficulty. I worked as a professor of literacy education at Kean University for 25 years, recently retiring in 2019.

Forever the student, 9 years ago I also began training for a second career—that of becoming a psychoanalyst. My reason for pursuing this path was that, although I felt well trained in understanding the cognitive aspects of people's lives, I felt deeply drawn to further understand, and to work with, the emotional aspects of their lives. I am pleased to share that I am now continuing to study and work as a psychotherapist at the Center for Modern Psychoanalytic Studies in, New York City. I find this new career deeply engaging and satisfying.

This book then is a summary, written explicitly for parents, of all that I feel is most valuable regarding how to help children overcome reading challenges. It is based on my 25 years as a university professor of literacy education and on my 9 years of training and work in the field of psychotherapy. I certainly hope that the book's contents will benefit you and your child.

About This Book

As I contemplated writing this book, I wondered if there would be a need for it. Surely there must be other books written on the topic, and an abundance of information available on the Internet? After investigation, I found that there really is no other book remotely similar to this one. There are some books that help you learn how to motivate your young child to want to become a reader (for example, *How to Raise a Reader*, Paul & Russo, 2019), and other books that help you strengthen a part of your child's reading skill set (for example, *The Next Step Forward in Word Study and Phonics*, Richardson & Dufresne, 2019), but there are no other books currently on the market that offer a comprehensive, theoretically grounded, linear and integrated approach to understanding, monitoring, and supporting your child's ability to overcome reading difficulty. Similarly, while there is a lot of information available online, virtually all of it is piecemeal, giving parents little understanding of the complexity inherent in reading success and guidance in how to best help their child achieve it.

In *Helping Your Child Overcome Reading Challenges*, I provide concise, easily understandable explanations of what ideally happens during the reading process, explorations of factors that frequently cause reading problems, checklists for determining your child's strengths and weaknesses in each of these areas, and ideas and resources for strengthening your child's identified area(s) of need. The goals of this book are to help you:

+ Understand the many factors that contribute to reading success.

+ Determine which factor, or factors, may be causing your child's reading difficulty.

+ Provide the targeted intervention and support for each area of your child's difficulty.

Overall, the intent of this book is to help you and your child negotiate the comprehensive journey of overcoming reading difficulty with the best possible experiences and outcomes.

There are multiple ways that you can read and use this book. For those of you who want an organized, linear understanding of the topic, I strongly encourage you to read it straight through. In the current chapter, I've introduced you to the topic of children's reading difficulty. In the next chapter, I present what I think of as the foundations of reading. The foundations of reading are based on the premise that *reading is primarily a cognitive activity and, therefore, anything that affects your child's brain will affect his reading. I highlight research findings on the relationships between brain function/reading achievement and nutrition, sleep, exercise, emotional well-being, and behavioral habits.* I also provide practical ideas for helping children achieve healthy patterns in all of these areas, so that optimal brain function can be the foundation of your child's journey to overcoming reading difficulty.

Chapter 2 addresses the foundational factors that affect brain function and consequently reading achievement, and Chapter 3 specifically examines the reading process. In Chapter 3, you will learn about the components of the PDPM, which serves as the organizational frame for the subsequent chapters. The components of the reading process introduced in Chapter 3 (and examined in depth throughout the book) are visual processing, auditory processing, phonics, vocabulary development, comprehension, metacognition, text difficulty, attention, and motivation. Chapter 4 explains the importance of understanding your child's abilities in each of these areas and features checklists that can be used to determine your child's strengths and difficulties. Once you have determined the area or areas in which your child needs additional support, Chapters 5 through 10 provide the information and guidance you'll need to help your child in those areas, as follows:

+ Chapter 5—for help with visual processing.

+ Chapter 6—for help with auditory processing.

+ Chapter 7—for help with phonics.

+ Chapter 8—for help with vocabulary development.

+ Chapter 9—for help with comprehension and metacognition.

+ Chapter 10—for help with text difficulty, attention, and motivation.

If you prefer not to read the book straight through, an alternative way to use the book is to start with Chapter 4, which features checklists that can determine your child's strengths and difficulties in all of the areas that affect reading success. Then, once you have determined which area(s) warrant additional support, you can turn directly to the chapter or chapters that affect those areas.

There are so many reasons to be hopeful about your child's future as a successful reader. First, there are numerous strategies and resources available to help you and your child overcome reading challenges, and this book features a great many of them. Second, as proof of one's potential to lead a successful life despite having reading challenges, some of the most famous people in the world have overcome this struggle. You'll find quotations from a few of them at the beginning of each chapter. Both you and your child may be inspired by the notable accomplishments of these individuals during their lives:

Leonardo da Vinci (artist and inventor)

George Washington (first president of the United States)

Benjamin Franklin (founding father of the United States)

Andrew Jackson (seventh president of the United States)

Charles Darwin (scientist)

Albert Einstein (scientist)

Pablo Picasso (artist)

Eleanor Roosevelt (former first lady of the United States)

Sir Winston Churchill (prime minister of the United Kingdom)

Lee Kuan Yew (first prime minister of Singapore)

Woodrow Wilson (28th president of the United States)

Dwight D. Eisenhower (34th president of the United States)

Lyndon B. Johnson (36th president of the United States)

George H. W. Bush (41st president of the United States)

George W. Bush (43rd president of the United States)

Henry Winkler (actor)

Steven Spielberg (filmmaker)

Caitlyn Jenner (Olympic gold medal–winning athlete)

Richard Branson (entrepreneur)

Tommy Hilfiger (designer)

Whoopi Goldberg (actor)

Tom Cruise (actor)

Anderson Cooper (journalist)

Octavia Spencer (actor)

Justin Timberlake (musician and actor)

Keira Knightley (actor)

Clearly, as this list of famous people abundantly attests, reading challenges can be overcome, and individuals can go forward to build fulfilling, self-actualized lives.

2

The Foundations of Reading

As you make your way along life's tumultuous highways, it's important to note that you should always carry a map, have plenty of fuel in the tank, and take frequent rest stops.

—OCTAVIA SPENCER (overcame a
reading difficulty to become an actor)

You might be surprised to find that the second chapter in a book written to help you help your child overcome reading difficulty is devoted to nutrition, sleep, exercise, emotions, and behaviors. I discuss these areas because *reading is basically a process that takes place in the brain,* and *nutrition, sleep, exercise, emotions, and behaviors all affect how well the brain works.* In other words, nutrition, sleep, exercise, emotions, and behaviors constitute the foundations upon which your child's reading skills are built. Just as the foundation of a house needs to be sturdy to support the walls, doors, windows, and roof, so do your child's nutrition, sleep, exercise, emotions, and behaviors need to be strong to support the optimal brain function needed for reading. This chapter helps you understand the role of these five areas in brain function and reading ability, and provides suggestions and resources to help your child overcome difficulties. The figure on the facing page depicts the foundational roles of these five areas in reading achievement as a pyramid. The literacy pyramid is similar to Maslow's hierarchy of needs, and I've found that it works well for literacy too.

Literacy Pyramid

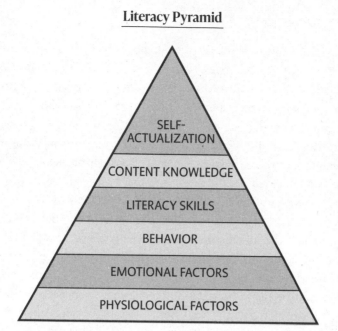

The Physiological Foundation

Nutrition

There is a strong and consistent body of research showing clear relationships between what children eat, how well their brains work, and academic achievement. The science behind this research shows that certain foods enhance brain development and connectivity (both are required for learning), while other foods impede brain development and connectivity. Research results on the connections between nutrition and school achievement are so strong and consistent that, in the 1960s, the United States started national school breakfast and lunch programs. Since then, researchers have more specifically articulated the details of nutrition that lead to optimal brain health and subsequently high academic achievement.

FOODS TO AVOID

First are the foods to avoid. As you might expect, these are foods that are high in chemical additives, such as preservatives and food colorings, and sugar, salt, and saturated fat. Foods high in chemicals, sugar, salt, and saturated fat create substances called *free radicals* in your child's body, which can damage brain cells. Free radicals also damage the synaptic relays in the brain responsible for transmitting information. Consumption of these substances is associated with lower school performance and increased rates of attention difficulties and learning disabilities. For examples of foods to avoid, see the box below. If you are unsure of whether or not a packaged food item is harmful for your child's brain health, look at the ingredients listed on the package. If you don't know what an ingredient is, or if you have trouble pronouncing it, it's best not to feed it to your child!

Researchers have also identified foods that strengthen brain health and that are subsequently associated with higher academic achievement. In general, a *whole-foods, plant-based* diet will provide a healthy foundation for your child's brain. The term *whole foods* means food that is *not processed. Nonprocessed* foods are those that are found in nature:

Examples of Foods to Avoid

Most packaged snack foods

Candy

Soda

Sweetened fruit juices

Power drinks

Prepared meal kits (such as macaroni and cheese)

Packaged sweets, such as cookies, crackers, and cakes

Many frozen food products

Processed meats, such as hot dogs, sausages, and bacon

---

vegetables, fruits, nuts, seeds, beans, and grains. Many of these foods are found in the produce aisles of grocery stores and can be eaten raw, cooked, or dried; all forms are healthy. These foods also form the core of a *plant-based diet* and are the main foods that you should feed your child. This diet can also incorporate small amounts of meat, dairy, and treats, but most of what your child eats should ideally be whole foods and plant based.

Nutrients that have been particularly well researched with regard to brain function and academic achievement are omega-3 fatty acids. Omega-3 fatty acids strengthen synaptic plasticity in the brain, and increased synaptic plasticity is closely linked to improved learning. In addition, *omega-3 fatty acid deficits have been linked to increased risks of attention-deficit disorder, dyslexia, and lower reading and writing achievement.* Omega-3 fatty acids are found in abundance in wild salmon (fresh, canned red and pink, and smoked), ground flax seeds and chia seeds (which can be added to shakes, smoothies, and soups), walnuts, and kiwifruit. One great way to improve your child's nutrition is to integrate omega-3 fatty acid foods into his or her diet. Additional ideas and resources are provided in the section on improving your child's nutrition that follows.

When discussing nutrition, it's also extremely important to pay attention to your child's hydration. Water is the ideal liquid for your child to drink, and sparkling water (also called seltzer or club soda) is equally good. Ideally, strive to have your child drink four to eight cups of water per day, with younger children needing less than older children. Adding a little fresh lemon or lime juice to sparkling water over ice is a healthy, refreshing, zero-calorie, inexpensive, and delicious substitute for sugary, processed drinks.

If you feel that your child's nutrition needs improvement, the following are 10 ideas that can help you make gradual changes in the direction of healthy eating that promotes optimal brain function.

10 IDEAS FOR IMPROVING YOUR CHILD'S NUTRITION

✦ *Establish a baseline.* To get an accurate sense of the food choices that you and your child are making, nutrition experts recommend tracking what your child is eating. To track food choices, simply write down everything that your child eats for breakfast, lunch, dinner, and snacks for a week. The purpose of this activity is to provide you and your child with information regarding current food choices.

✦ *Make an improvement plan.* Once you have completed a week's worth of food tracking, work with your child to develop a plan for improvement. Ideally, the improvement plan will be gradual, realistic, and account for any particular family needs. A sample 4-week nutrition improvement plan is provided in the box on pages 17–18.

✦ *Include your child in planning, and explain why you are making changes.* Another idea for improving your child's nutrition is to include him in meal planning. Your child can help pick meals for the week, construct a shopping list, find items in the store, read recipes, and cook with you. All of these activities will improve your child's nutrition, reading, and food preparation skills.

> "Parents should make mealtimes a priority. During this time, children should be focused on having conversations at the table rather than watching television or being on electronic devices. Allowing children to be on a device while eating leads to mindless eating. Children thrive on routine, and they will feel safe knowing there will be a scheduled time to have a meal with their family each day. This will allow children to have a positive relationship with food."
>
> —Ashley Quinn, first-grade teacher

✦ *Model excellent nutrition.* Needless to say, your child learns much from watching you and other adults and siblings in the house. Your child's nutritional improvements have the greatest chance of becoming permanent when everyone in the household adopts the same changes.

✦ *Join one or more online support groups.* Online support groups for whole-food, plant-based eating are a great way to increase your knowledge base and to find recipes.

✦ *Keep learning.* Many other sources for learning about whole-food, plant-based eating exist. These include videos on *YouTube* and recipes on *Instagram.* Some of my favorite books on the topic are: *The China Study,*

Sample Nutrition Improvement Plan

Week 1: Make a conscious decision to improve the quality of your child's breakfasts. If cereal is a favorite choice, change from a cereal high in sugar, food coloring, and/or additives to one that is whole grain, low sugar, and organic. Consider changing from dairy milk to a plant-based milk, such as oat milk or almond milk. Add fresh fruit to every breakfast. Most children love bananas, apples, oranges, grapes, pears, plums, strawberries, blueberries, raspberries, watermelon, kiwifruit, mango, and cherries. Consider smoothies part of your child's breakfast routine. Smoothies can start with a plant-based milk, such as oat milk, and then a variety of fruits and vegetables can be blended in. *Add one teaspoon of ground flaxseed to your child's breakfast cereal and/or breakfast smoothie for an omega-3 fatty acid boost. Whenever your budget and access allow, buy organic.* Also consider adding some nuts or seeds to your child's breakfast.

Week 2: Keep the changes accomplished in week 1 and, in addition, make a conscious decision to improve the quality of your child's lunches. Aim for two servings of vegetables, one serving of fruit, one serving of whole grains, and one serving of protein for lunch each day. Vegetables that most children will eat raw include carrots, celery, cucumbers, red and yellow peppers, and sugar snap peas. Whole-grain sources include whole-grain bread and wraps, brown rice, quinoa, and whole-grain pasta. Protein sources include peanut butter (and other nut butters), hummus, beans, dairy, eggs, tofu, poultry, beef, and fish.

Week 3: Keep the changes accomplished in weeks 1 and 2 and, in addition, make a conscious decision to improve the quality of your child's dinners. As with lunch, aim for two servings of vegetables, one serving of fruit, one serving of whole grains, and one serving of protein for dinner each day. Soups and stews are a great way to get children to eat their vegetables, grains, and proteins. Since children often object to eating green, leafy vegetables, which are great for their brain health, try blending them into your soups, stews, and pasta sauce. Likewise, leafy greens and beans can be chopped up into taco mixtures.

Another way to facilitate vegetable consumption, for instance, is to make cauliflower wings in the oven or an air fryer. There are lots of recipes available on the Internet for this delicious chicken wing substitute. Similarly, homemade potato and sweet potato fries are filled with nutrients, while their packaged counterparts are often laden with brain-harming chemicals. Last, don't forget corn on the cob! Many children love this delicious, healthy, and low-cost vegetable.

Week 4: Keep the changes accomplished in weeks 1, 2, and 3 and, in addition, make a conscious decision to improve the quality of your child's snacks. Snacks are often the weakest link in children's diet; however, with commitment and planning, healthier snack choices can become the new norm. As with breakfast, lunch, and dinner, the goal with healthy snacking is to eat as much food as possible in its natural, plant-based form. Here is a list of healthy foods that many children will be agreeable to trying: fresh fruit (bananas, apples, oranges, grapes, pears, plums, strawberries, blueberries, raspberries, watermelon, kiwi, mango, and cherries); raw vegetables (carrots, celery, cucumbers, red and yellow peppers, and sugar snap peas); dried fruit (raisins, cranberries, apricots, and mango); all-natural popcorn; and homemade potato, sweet potato, and kale chips. If your child insists on cookies, cake, candy, and ice cream, try to choose brands that are organic and low in sugar and fat.

written by a former Cornell University professor of nutrition and his son (Campbell & Campbell, 2006); *How Not to Die*, written by a brilliant physician and founder of Nutritionfacts.org (Greger, 2015); *Forks over Knives*, a #1 *New York Times* best seller (Stone, 2011); and *Fiber Fueled* created by a gastroenterologist (Bulsiewicz, 2020).

✦ *Track progress.* Improving the ways in which your child and you and your family eat may, or may not, constitute a big change. Either way, it can be helpful to track progress. Which days and times are the easiest to adhere to healthy eating? Which ones are the hardest?

✦ *Focus on progress, not perfection.* Since none of us are perfect, setting perfection as a goal invariably leads to failure and self-criticism. Instead, help your child learn to focus on progress. Did he eat five healthy breakfasts this past week? That's great! Can he try for the same number next week?

✦ *Celebrate success.* If your child's nutrition has been far from ideal in the past, adopting a whole-food, plant-based diet will be a big change. Help your child celebrate small and incremental successes in ways that are meaningful to her.

✦ *Flexibility and kindness.* Learning to eat a healthy whole-food, plant-based diet can take years. Proceed with flexibility and kindness for your child, yourself, and others.

Sleep

Just as there is a clear body of research linking what we eat to optimal brain function, there is an equally compelling body of research showing connections between sleep and brain function. This research strongly indicates that if you want to maximize your child's brain function, school performance, and academic/reading achievement, helping him get a good night's sleep every night is imperative. The theoretical mechanism underlying these research findings is called *sleep-dependent memory consolidation*. This concept suggests that specific biological processes take place during sleep that actually consolidate memories and learning. The biological process that support this theory is the growing of dendritic spines. Dendritic spines are docking stations in the brain that allow neurons to connect—the biological equivalent of learning. Dendritic spines grow during sleep (and do not grow in the absence of sleep).

In case you were wondering about the ideal amount of sleep for your child, the American Academy of Pediatrics provides the following guidelines:

✦ Infants 4–12 months: 12–16 hours per 24 hours, including naps

✦ 1- to 2-year-old children: 11–14 hours per 24 hours, including naps

✦ 3- to 5-year-old children: 10–13 hours per 24 hours, including naps

✦ 6- to 12-year-old children: 9–12 hours per 24 hours

✦ 13- to 18-year-olds: 8–10 hours per 24 hours

Underscoring the critical importance of sleep to learning, the National Foundation for the Centers for Disease Control and Prevention has labeled the extent of sleep deprivation in the United States to be a public health epidemic. The following are some ideas that can help your child get the sleep that she needs every night.

To develop good sleep habits in your child, *begin by removing (or at least minimizing) the things that interfere with falling, and staying, asleep.* First remove drinks and food with caffeine, sugar, and chemicals from your child's diet, or at least minimize their consumption after lunch. Second, remove or minimize the use of television and electronics at least an hour before your child's bedtime. Television and electronics typically stimulate the brain. To facilitate sleep we want to do the opposite: calm and quiet the brain. Third, as much as possible, try to reduce external activities, noise, and distractions while your child is trying to fall asleep or is asleep. I understand that these guidelines can be difficult to implement in busy homes, but I also know that they can help your child get the sleep that he needs for his brain to be at its best for learning the next day.

In addition to removing anything that interferes with falling and staying asleep, there are steps that you can take to enhance your child's ability to fall asleep and stay asleep. Probably most important are setting a consistent bedtime for your child and creating a consistent before-bed routine. It is helpful for your child to know his bedtime. His bedtime routine should start about 45 minutes before you want your child to be asleep. Begin with a warm bath or shower for your child, followed by several bedtime stories that you either read to or tell your child. To make life simple, it's a good idea to keep the number of stories steady; maybe consider reading two books to your child when the lights are low and then telling your child one story when the lights are out. Children typically enjoy hearing stories about their own families, and they frequently enjoy hearing the same ones over and over. In addition to setting a consistent bedtime and bedtime routine, playing quiet music, using soothing lotions like lavender, and turning on a dim night-light may make your child's transition to sleep an easier and more pleasant one.

In addition to these suggestions, you may want to browse the HealthStatus.com website. This website has a great assortment of articles, including *How to Help a Child with School Anxiety Sleep Well, Sleep Strategies for Kids,* and *How Blue Light* [screen time] *Affects Kids' Sleep.*

Exercise

A third foundational area that significantly contributes to your child's brain health is daily exercise. Research benefits associated with regular exercise for children include improved grades, standardized test scores, attention, and memory. It is believed that these gains are a result of increased blood and oxygen flow to the brain that takes place during exercise and also to increased brain synaptic plasticity associated with exercise.

Given the scientific evidence regarding the positive correlations between physical exercise, academic achievement, and brain function, the current state of exercise among American youth is deeply disturbing, because research indicates that physical activity levels among children and adolescents have significantly dropped over the past several decades. In addition, the National Foundation for the Centers for Disease Control and Prevention has determined that only about 30% of American children reach the recommended benchmark of 60 minutes (continuous or noncontinuous) of moderate to vigorous physical activity per day.

If your child is one of the 70% of American children that does not attain this daily recommended benchmark goal, inactivity may be contributing to your child's reading difficulty. Here are a few ideas for improving your child's level of physical activity:

✦ *Establish a baseline.* Begin by helping your child understand the connection between physical activity, brain function, and academic achievement and track your child's physical activity for a week as a baseline.

✦ *Create an improvement plan.* Create an improvement plan with your child, with the goal of 60 minutes a day of physical activity. If needed, slowly work up to this goal with a 6-week plan.

✦ *Consider outdoor activities that you can do with your child.* Often exercising with your child is the best route to helping her get more active. Can you and your child take a walk together every evening after dinner? Can you bike or hike together on Saturdays? Jog together on Sundays? Play basketball? Practice with a soccer ball? All of these activities will benefit your child's (and your) brain health.

✦ *Consider indoor activities that you can do with your child.* Sometimes outdoor exercise is not an option. In these situations, consider indoor activities that you can enjoy together. One easy way to do this is to simply type "Exercise for Kids" into YouTube. Many free workout videos will pop up. A few that I found are *10-Minute Family Fun Cardio Exercise Workout, Cardio Workout for Kids and Adults* (25 minutes), *10 Fun Daily Exercises for Kids to Do at Home* (10 minutes), *Kids Workout 1 Beginners* (16 minutes), and *Best Kids Exercise Video Workout at Home* (23 minutes).

✦ *Consider activities that your child can do without you.* Although one of the best ways to get your child active is to be active with him, another approach is to help your child participate in exercise activities with other children. Here are a few activities that your child may be willing to try with his peers: soccer, softball/baseball, basketball, gymnastics, swimming, climbing, hiking, skating, skiing, and track.

✦ *Track progress.* Given that 70% of American children do not engage in 60 minutes of daily physical activity, it is likely that your child needs help persevering with this important physiological foundation of brain health. Focus on progress (not perfection!), and for the best results possible, join your child in tracking her progress and staying active.

The Emotional Foundation

The connections between emotions, brain function, and reading achievement are grounded in an understanding that all parts of the brain affect each other. Therefore, although the part of the brain that regulates emotions (the limbic system) is different from the parts of the brain located in the cerebrum that are used during reading, the functioning of the cerebrum is affected by changes in the limbic system. More specifically, affective neuroscience (the neuroscientific study of emotions) clearly shows that changes in emotion affect cognition. Consistent with the understanding that emotions affect cognition, research indicates that as students' stress levels increase, their academic performance decreases. Unfortunately, in today's world, there are numerous potential sources of stress in children's lives, including conflict within the family, separation of parents, divorce, illness, death, financial stress, job loss, moving, incarceration, deportation, domestic violence, sexual abuse, addiction, and the birth of a sibling. Even struggling with reading itself can be a source of stress for children.

Because children experience so many potential sources of stress and because emotional stress has a detrimental effect on children's brain function and reading achievement, it is advisable to consider therapeutic ways to respond if your child is experiencing emotional distress. The following time-tested ideas are well regarded in the field of child psychology.

✦ *Differentiate between your child's feelings and behaviors.* Often when children are upset and stressed, you will see negative behaviors emerge. Children may become uncooperative and oppositional. You may see them act out by not following rules, "talking back," and even hitting, kicking, and/or biting siblings and friends. When you see these kinds of behaviors, *before intervening,* think about what feelings your child might be having that are driving such behaviors. Is there a lot of tension in the home? Is your child frustrated because of having difficulty at school? Is something frightening happening in your child's life? *Trying to understand the feelings that are driving your child's behavior is the first step in helping your child manage his feelings (and behavior).* It may be helpful to remember that *your child is not giving you a hard time; your child is having a hard time!* Focusing on the feelings that are driving your child's behavior is the first critically important step in helping him manage his emotions.

✦ *Ask permission to speak with your child.* Once you have a sense of what feelings your child may be experiencing, it is helpful to try to open the lines of communication with him. So as not to be experienced as emotionally intrusive by your child, it is ideal to ask your child if it's OK to speak with him about what you're observing. An example of this type of communication is "I noticed that you seem to be having trouble following the rules today. Is it OK if we talk about this?" Another example is "I noticed that you seemed upset today. Is it OK if we talk about this?" If your child says "yes," you can proceed with the ideas that follow. If your child says "no," try to accept his need to not talk. Let your child know that you are there for him when he is ready to speak. You can say, "I understand. I just want you to know that I care about how you're feeling and doing. If you change your mind, please know that I'm here for you." You can also suggest that, if your child isn't ready to talk about what is bothering him, he can communicate with you about it via a card, letter, email, text, or even a picture.

✦ *Open the lines of communication with your child.* Assuming your child is willing to speak with you, it's useful to begin the conversation by asking your child to *help you understand* what she is experiencing. An example of this kind of communication is "It seems to me that you're having a hard time today. Can you help me understand what you think might be going on?" Shifting your communication in this way allows your child to become the expert on what she is experiencing. It also helps you remember to consider your child's perspective on what is occurring.

✦ *If your child explains his understanding of the situation, see if he can generate any possible solutions.* You might say something like "Do you have any ideas about what we can do that would help you feel better about that?" If your child does have ideas, discuss them with him. If your child doesn't have any ideas, you can again ask, "Is it OK if I offer an idea of what might help?" Again, questioning your child in these ways gives him the opportunity to practice independent problem-solving skills. These techniques also illustrate that you're respecting your child as he matures.

✦ *If your child can't explain her understanding of the situation, ask if you can offer an interpretation of what may be problematic.* Sometimes your child will not be able to identify what is upsetting her. If this is the case, perhaps you as the parent have an idea. If so, you can ask, "Is it OK if I tell you what I think the problem might be?" Again, questioning in this way allows your child to be empowered regarding what is being discussed. Sometimes your child will say "yes," and a discussion between the two of you can ensue. At other times your child will say "no." If this happens, you can revert to the communication already described: "I understand. I just want you to know that I care about how you're feeling and doing. If you change your mind, please know that I'm here for you."

In addition to these ideas, you may want to learn more about ways to help your child understand and manage her feelings. Here are a few extra resources:

+ Naturalchild.org: "Emotions Are Not Bad Behavior"
+ *My Mixed Emotions: Help Your Kids Handle Their Feelings* (Healy, 2018)
+ *The Whole-Brain Child: 12 Revolutionary Strategies to Nurture Your Child's Developing Mind* (Siegel, 2012)
+ *Raising a Secure Child: How Circle of Security Parenting Can Help You Nurture Your Child's Attachment, Emotional Resilience, and Freedom to Explore* (Hoffman, Cooper, Powell, & Benton, 2017)
+ *Anxious Ninja: A Children's Book about Managing Anxiety and Difficult Emotions* (Nhin, 2020)

To conclude this section on helping your child manage his emotions, here are a few of my favorite emotionally therapeutic things to say to children:

"I'm grateful for you."

"You don't have to be perfect to be great."

"I love you."

"Your opinions matter to me."

"You can say no."

"You are right."

"We can try it your way."

"That's a great question."

"That was a really good choice."

"I can tell you're trying really hard."

"I appreciate you."

"Everyone makes mistakes."

"Sometimes things are really hard."

"Sometimes life is really hard."

"I'm here for you."

The Behavioral Foundation

To achieve academically, students need to be able to focus and pay attention to the learning tasks at hand. Applying what we know about nutrition, sleep, exercise, and managing difficult emotions will greatly help your
child improve her attention and focus. In addition, your child may need
help in managing behaviors that interfere with learning. Some problematic behaviors that often accompany reading difficulty are oppositional
behaviors (for example, an unwillingness to cooperate in matters related
to learning and/or a variety of daily living activities); avoidant behaviors
(such as avoiding reading and writing activities); tantrums (displays of
extreme distress, including screaming, crying, and flailing arms and legs);
and violent behaviors (such as hitting and biting others, as well as self-
harming behavior). Even though I, of course, support working with your
child on any behavior that may be problematic, if your child is engaged
in any violent and/or self-harming activity (for example, self-cutting and/
or drug, alcohol, tobacco, or food abuse), I strongly recommend that you
confer with a professional. In addition, the following ideas and resources
can help you help your child develop the behaviors that are needed to
facilitate reading achievement.

+ *Differentiate between your child's feelings and behaviors.* Yes, this
point has already been discussed, but it's such an important one that it
needs to be emphasized again. If you feel that your child's behavior problem is being driven by upset emotions (*which is almost always the case*),
refer back to the guidelines in the section "The Emotional Foundation."
If you feel that your child's behavior needs to be shaped using behavioral
modification techniques in addition to working with her feelings, continue reading the suggestions that follow.

+ *Establish a baseline.* Begin by tracking your child's problem behavior (or behaviors) for a week or two. Which behaviors are problematic?

When do the problems seem to arise? When do they seem better or worse? What seems to increase versus decrease the intensity of the problem(s)?

+ *Create an improvement plan.* Create an improvement plan, ideally in collaboration with your child. Help your child understand that mastering the problematic behavior or behaviors will help him become a better student and reader. I suggest targeting one behavior at a time rather than multiple problematic behaviors at once. For example, if your child is having difficulties in the areas of not following rules, refusing to practice reading, and fighting with his brother, develop an improvement plan that focuses on the first problem for 6 weeks, then on the second problem for the next 6 weeks, and so forth.

+ *When targeting a problematic behavior, focus on gradual improvement, not perfection.* Anytime our children (or we) are facing a challenge, it is best to focus on improvement rather than perfection, as improvement is almost always possible, while perfection almost never is. For example, in this case, in week 1, see if your child can follow all of the family rules from morning until noon. In week 2, see if she can follow all of the rules until 3:00 P.M. In week 3, see if she can follow all of the rules until 5:00 P.M., and so on.

+ *Use rewards with care.* Here again I want to emphasize my strong belief that childhood behavior problems should ideally be dealt with by working with your child's feelings that are driving the problematic behavior, as previously described in "The Emotional Foundation" section. If, along with helping your child manage his feelings, he also needs help shaping his behavior, you can reward behaviors that you're trying to strengthen. When using rewards, there are a few guidelines that will enhance their effectiveness: (1) When deciding how often to give rewards, the further the actual behavior is from the desired behavior, the shorter the duration should be between rewards. For example, if your child is only able to stay in his chair for 5 minutes at a time, begin by giving a reward every time he can stay in the chair for 6 minutes. Gradually increase the time between rewards to every 7 minutes and so forth, until he can stay in his chair and work for 30 minutes at a sitting. (2) Make sure that the reward you are using is actually appealing to your child. Time on the computer or iPad is one treat that most children really enjoy.

(3) Minimize the use of rewards as soon as your child is able to connect to the good feelings associated with success. The reason for tapering rewards, as much as possible, is that it will be helpful to your child to be able to use his own good feelings as a source of satisfaction as he grows older.

In addition to these ideas and resources, you may want to learn more about ways to help your child with her behavior(s). Here are a few extra resources:

+ *Beyond Behaviors: Using Brain Science and Compassion to Understand and Solve Children's Behavioral Challenges* (Delahooke, 2019)

+ *Smart but Scattered: The Revolutionary "Executive Skills" Approach to Helping Kids Reach Their Potential* (Dawson & Guare, 2009)

+ *Parenting Toolbox: 125 Activities Therapists Use to Reduce Meltdowns, Increase Positive Behaviors, and Manage Emotions* (Phifer, Sibbald, & Roden, 2018)

+ *What Should Danny Do?* (Levy & Levy, 2018)

+ Childmind.org: "Managing Problem Behavior at Home"

Chapter Highlights

This book is based on the premise that nutrition, sleep, exercise, emotions, and behavior all affect brain function and therefore also affect your child's reading ability. This chapter details the role of these factors in brain function and reading ability, and provides ideas and resources for helping your child develop optimal patterns in each of these areas.

3

The Parts
of the Reading Process

Continuous effort—not strength or intelligence—is the
key to unlocking our potential.

—SIR WINSTON CHURCHILL (overcame
a reading difficulty to become prime
minister of the United Kingdom)

Chapter 2 explored three levels of foundations that undergird your child's brain function and reading ability: physiological well-being (nutrition, sleep, and exercise), emotional well-being, and behavioral well-being. Strengths in these areas will enhance your child's ability to read, while problems in these areas will impede his ability to read. This chapter focuses on understanding the reading process itself. Examining how the reading process and its constituent parts work provides a deeper and clearer understanding of what needs to happen for your child to read easily and well.

The model of reading presented in this chapter is known as the *parallel distributed processing model* (PDPM). Key elements of the model were developed by researchers in the 1980s and then subsequently detailed in a nearly 500-page book entitled *Beginning to Read: Thinking and Learning about Print* (Adams, 1990). Today, many reading professionals consider this model to be the best one for explaining what happens during the reading process.

The PDPM conceptualizes reading as taking place in four interconnected processors in the brain: the orthographic processor, the phonological processor, the meaning processor, and the context processor. Each of these processors is responsible for a specific part of the reading process, and each one also sends and receives information from the others. A visual depiction of the PDPM is presented below, and a description of how each processor works to create the integrated experience of reading is described in the sections that follow.

The Orthographic Processor and Visual Processing

In the PDPM, reading is conceptualized as starting in the orthographic processor, the place where print is perceived and processed. As readers grow in proficiency, a system called the *interletter associational unit system* evolves. This system acts like a small computer in the brain, in that every

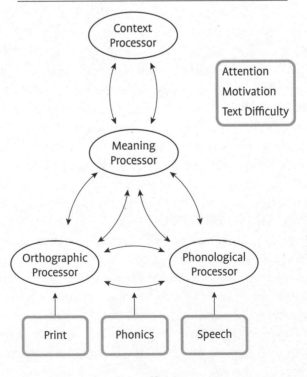

Modeling the Reading System: Four Processors

time a target letter is perceived, the system activates letters that are likely to follow the target letter and suppresses letters that are unlikely to follow the target letter. Despite its long name, the interletter associational unit system is easy to understand if you think about how your smartphone works. When you type the letter *H* at the beginning of a word on your phone, your phone generates the next letter *i* because *H* followed by *i* is the most common spelling used when texting. The system functions in the same way in the brain during reading and, when it works well, it allows readers to easily and quickly process print. Keep in mind, however that the system is activated only when a reader's letter recognition is instantaneous. This underscores the importance of young children having automatic letter recognition skill. In the absence of instantaneous letter recognition, the entire interletter associational unit system will fail to ignite, and the reader will be left reading "letter by letter."

You can use the Visual Processing Checklist in Chapter 4 (pages 44–45) to determine if your child may be having difficulty with her orthographic processor. If so, you can then read Chapter 5 to learn more about visual processing and how to help your child in this area with activities and resources.

The Phonological Processor and Auditory Processing

The phonological processor is the second key processor in the PDPM. While visual processing (the processing of print) takes place in the orthographic processor, auditory processing (the processing of sounds) takes place in the phonological processor. Highly skilled processing of sounds is essential for reading success. *Weakness in the phonological processor is the most common cause of reading difficulty*, and is particularly common among children who have, or who have had, frequent ear infections.

The processing of sounds occurs at multiple levels in the phonological processor. From the easiest to the most complex to learn, they are: (1) the ability to hear individual words within sentences, (2) the ability to rhyme, (3) the ability to hear the beginning sounds of words, (4) the ability to hear the ending sounds of words, and (5) the ability to hear the middle sounds in words.

You can use the Auditory Processing Checklist in Chapter 4 (pages 45–46) to determine if the phonological processor may be the source of your child's difficulty. If so, you can then read Chapter 6 to find out more about auditory processing and about the activities and resources that can help your child in this area.

Phonics

Phonics refers to the ability to match letters (print) and sounds. Phonics ability is a central component of the reading process (but certainly not the only important component). Although not identified as a distinct processor in the PDPM, the diagram on page 30 shows phonics as the point of intersection between the orthographic and phonological processors. Using this diagram, one can see that, if a reader is having difficulty in either processing print (in the orthographic processor) or in processing sounds (in the phonological processor), the accurate matching of print and sound (phonics) will be impeded. Therefore, if your child is having difficulty in phonics, it is imperative that you also determine whether visual and/or auditory problems are contributing to the phonics difficulty.

You can use the Phonics Skills Checklist in Chapter 4 (pages 47–48) to determine if your child is having difficulty with phonics. If so, you can then read Chapter 7 to learn more about phonics and how to help your child in this area with activities and resources. Be sure to also assess your child's visual and auditory processing skills if your child is having difficulty with phonics, because underlying problems in these areas can present as phonics difficulty. As already noted, Chapter 4 can help you with assessment in these areas, and Chapters 5 and 6 provide helpful visual- and auditory-processing interventions if needed.

The Low-Level Processors

The orthographic processor, the phonological processor, and the phonics component are known as the *low-level processors* of the PDPM, as shown in their physical locations in the diagram on page 30. The low-level processors have a very important job in the reading process: *they work together to help readers identify words.* These processors help readers recognize words but are not involved with helping them understand the meaning of words or comprehend the message of the text (the processors responsible for these skills are described next). The low-level processors "simply" process print, sounds, and the matching of print and sounds, so that readers can identify individual words as they read. Accurate and efficient word identification, which takes place in the low-level processors, is a central factor in the reading process and often takes much of a reader's internal attention.

The Meaning Processor and Vocabulary Knowledge

The meaning processor, located in the middle of the PDPM, is responsible for attaching meanings to words after the words have been identified by the low-level processors. Stated another way, the low-level processors are responsible for accurate word identification, and the meaning processor is responsible for adding accurate word meanings after each word has been identified.

The content of the meaning processor (word meanings) is organized in the brain according to *schemata* (plural of *schema*). A schema is everything that a person knows about a particular topic. For example, a person's schema for hiking is everything that a person knows about hiking, and a person's schema for cooking is everything that a person knows about cooking. People have schemata for nouns (for instance, cats, dinosaurs, beaches, cities, museums, zoos); verbs (for example, skiing, skating, napping, baking, writing); adjectives (for instance, funny, traumatic, lonely, tall); and adverbs (such as slowly, quickly, carefully, carelessly). Individuals vary greatly in the degree to which their schemata are elaborated. A professional skier naturally has a much more elaborated schema on the subject of skiing than someone who has only taken a few skiing lessons. Moreover, a person who has taken only a few skiing lessons has a much more elaborated schema on the subject than someone who has never skied at all. This information is all relevant to reading because *the more background information (schemata) a reader has on a topic, the easier it will be for that reader to read and comprehend texts on that subject.* In other words, the more elaborated any child's background schema, the more easily he will be able to read and comprehend texts on that subject.

You can use the Vocabulary Skills Checklist in Chapter 4 (pages 48–49) to determine if the meaning processor may be the source of your child's difficulty. If so, you can then read Chapter 8 for more information about vocabulary and schemata and about the activities and resources that can help your child in this area.

The Context Processor and Comprehension

The context processor is located at the top of the PDPM (see the diagram on page 30) and is the place where comprehension takes place. Comprehension is the ability to understand what is being read, and it's typically considered the goal of reading. When the context processor is working well, three activities take place in its neural networks: (1) it constructs the message as the reader reads, (2) it monitors whether or not the reader is understanding what is being read, and (3) it deploys fix-up strategies if the reader realizes that he does not understand what he is reading.

The first job of the context processor is to construct the message as the reader reads. The context processor does this by taking each word identified by the low-level processors, adding the word meanings provided by the meaning processor, and assembling the message into coherent units such as sentences, paragraphs, pages, chapters, and books.

As the context processor cumulatively constructs meaning from the text, it also monitors whether or not the reader comprehends what he is reading. This form of thinking is known as *metacognition*, which refers to a reader's ability to think about his own thinking. Metacognition is experienced by the reader as an internal voice during reading when the reader realizes, "Hey—wait a minute; I don't know what's going on here!" When the metacognitive dimension of the context processor is working well, the reader will be alerted that he is not comprehending the text and that something should be done to correct the problem.

The third job of the context processor is to deploy fix-up strategies when the reader realizes that he is not adequately comprehending the text. Fix-up strategies include behaviors such as slowing down and rereading difficult text; looking up unknown words; reorienting oneself to the current chapter, headings, and subheadings; and using pictures and charts for clues to comprehension.

You can use the Comprehension and Metacognition Checklist in Chapter 4 (pages 49–50) to determine if the context processor may be the source of your child's difficulty. If so, you can then read Chapter 9 for more information about comprehension and metacognition, as well as about the activities and resources that can help your child in this area.

Connectionism

All of the processors in the PDPM work according to the principle of *connectionism*. Connectionism is a belief system regarding the ways in which neural systems are organized in the brain. Connectionism indicates that all learning occurs as a result of connections in the brain, and that the more often any items are connected, the stronger and faster their connections become. When applied to literacy, connectionism shows that the more often someone reads, the stronger and faster her reading skills will become. In the language of connectionism, neural networks become faster and stronger as a result of repeated pairings. In more common language, connectionism indicates that practice makes perfect, as long as the reader is repeating correct connections.

Limited Internal Attention, Text Difficulty, and Motivation

Another underlying principle of the PDPM is that all readers have *limited internal attention*, which means that we all have a limit to how much information we can simultaneously process at any given time. When applied to reading, limited internal attention suggests that, if a reader is using a great deal of his internal attention in the low-level processors to identify words, it's likely he will not have sufficient remaining internal attention for his context processor to construct and monitor the meaning of the text. This phenomenon is often seen in struggling readers, who will tell you that they "read" the entire text but that they didn't understand it. If your child is one of these readers, it is likely that he is using too much of his internal attention to identify words and consequently does not have enough internal attention remaining to construct and monitor (comprehend) the meaning of the text. If this problem feels familiar to you, the solution lies in providing your child with an easier-level text to read. When you give your child texts to read that are at his correct independent reading level, less internal attention is needed for word identification, freeing up more internal attention for comprehension processes. In addition, motivation plays a big role in reading success.

You can use the reading-level guidelines and the Attention and Motivation Checklists in Chapter 4 (pages 52–53) to determine if your child may be having difficulties in these areas. You can read Chapter 10 for more information about the concepts of attention, text difficulty, and motivation, and about the activities and resources that can help your child in these areas.

The PDPM as a Diagnostic Tool

The PDPM is not only a great tool for deepening our understanding of what ideally takes place during the reading process, it is also a great tool for identifying the area or areas that may be causing one or more reading problems for your child. The PDPM allows us to put a metaphoric magnifying glass on each part of your child's reading process—the low-level processors (visual processing, auditory processing, and phonics); the meaning processor; the context processor; and the components of attention, reading level, and motivation—to determine how well that part of the process is functioning. If there are problems in one or more areas, specifically targeted interventions, as described in the upcoming chapters, can then be implemented. When the PDPM is used as a diagnostic tool in combination with assessments of the underlying foundations of your child's reading ability—nutrition, sleep, exercise, emotions, and behaviors, discussed in Chapter 2—a clearer understanding of your child's area(s) of difficulty will become evident, and a path for intervention and achievement can be pursued.

Weaknesses in Multiple Processors

A final thought to keep in mind regarding the PDPM is that children vary in the degree to which they have difficulty reading. Some children have only mild difficulty in a single processor, while others have more severe deficits in one or more processors. In general, the more processors in which your child is experiencing difficulty, the more difficult it will be to help her read easily and well. *Please be assured that having a more serious problem does not mean that it is impossible for your child to read easily and well!* While a reading problem caused by difficulties in multiple processors (and/or in multiple foundational areas) will most likely need greater attention and a longer period of time to remediate than problems that occur in only a single processor or single foundational area, correctly targeted, high-quality interventions implemented with care and persistence will enable virtually all children to eventually become successful readers.

Chapter Highlights

The model of reading presented in this chapter is known as the parallel distributed processing model (PDPM). The PDPM conceptualizes reading as taking place in four interconnected processors in the brain: the orthographic processor, where the visual processing of print occurs; the phonological processor, where the auditory processing of sound occurs; the meaning processor, where vocabulary meanings are attached to identified words; and the context processor, where the construction, comprehension, and metacognitive monitoring of the text message occurs. In addition, print and sounds are matched through phonics, which leads to word identification in the low-level processors of the model. The entire model is organized according to the principles of connectionism, and attention, text difficulty, and motivation all further affect reading success. The PDPM provides a visual representation for understanding what needs to happen during reading for word identification and text comprehension to occur easily and efficiently. Moreover, using the PDPM as a diagnostic tool allows educators and parents to identify deficits in specific processors, thereby illuminating the path for targeted, effective intervention. Chapter 4 describes how to assess your child's PDPM processors, related factors, and the underlying physiological, emotional, and behavioral foundations. Once you have completed assessing your child, you can read the related subsequent chapter to learn about the areas that need attention, and to locate activities and resources for strengthening them.

4

How Can I Tell What's Causing My Child's Reading Difficulty?

The difference between a strong man and a weak one is
that the former does not give up after a defeat.

> —WOODROW WILSON (overcame
> reading difficulty to become the 28th
> president of the United States)

As you have probably realized from reading the first three chapters of this book, becoming a successful reader can be a complicated process. To start, the foundations of reading (nutrition, sleep, exercise, emotional well-being, and behaviors, discussed in Chapter 2) all need to be considered when a child is experiencing reading difficulty. Then, the cognitive aspects of reading (visual processing, auditory processing, phonics, vocabulary, comprehension, metacognition, attention, motivation, and reading level, discussed in Chapter 3) should be examined. The present chapter helps you determine

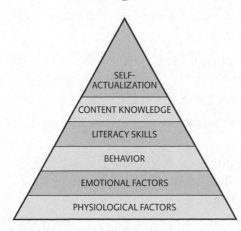

whether your child is having difficulty in one or more of the areas that contribute to reading success. I suggest that you read through the entire chapter to familiarize yourself with its contents. Afterward, you may want to complete one or more of the checklists with your child. Once you identify any areas in which your child is experiencing difficulty, use the upcoming chapters to learn more about those topics and to find activities and resources to help your child in those areas.

Monitoring Your Child's Physiological Well-Being

Nutrition, sleep, and exercise provide the necessary physiological foundation for your child's reading success because these three factors all affect how well the brain works. The guidelines in the following checklists can help in determining whether your child may be experiencing difficulty in one or more of these areas. If you find that your child is having difficulty in any of the areas listed in the checklists, use the information in Chapter 2 to support your child's improvement.

NUTRITION CHECKLIST. A check mark in any of these categories suggests that your child may benefit from improved nutrition. Refer to Chapter 2 to find out how to help your child in this important foundational area of reading success.

- ❑ My child's pediatrician has told me that my child needs help improving his nutrition.
- ❑ My child's pediatrician has told me that my child is overweight, underweight, or at an unhealthy weight or body mass index.
- ❑ My child is diabetic or prediabetic.
- ❑ My child regularly eats sugary cereal for breakfast or skips breakfast.
- ❑ My child regularly eats processed food (that is, food packaged in a box or bag that has more than one ingredient) for breakfast, lunch, and/or dinner.

❑ My child regularly drinks soda and/or other highly sweetened beverages.

❑ My child regularly eats processed food for snacks.

❑ My child regularly eats highly sweetened snacks, such as candy.

❑ My child eats fewer than three servings of fruit per day.

❑ My child eats fewer than three servings of vegetables per day.

❑ My child drinks less than three cups of water per day.

SLEEP CHECKLIST. A check mark in any of these categories suggests that your child may benefit from improved sleep habits. Refer to Chapter 2 to find out how to help your child in this important foundational area of reading success.

❑ My child's pediatrician has told me that my child needs help improving her sleep habits.

❑ My child's teacher has told me that my child often seems tired in school.

❑ My child often seems tired.

❑ My child regularly wakes up during the night.

❑ My child gets less than the amount of sleep recommended by the American Academy of Pediatrics:

- 4–12 months: 12–16 hours per 24 hours, including naps
- 1–2 years: 11–14 hours per 24 hours, including naps
- 3–5 years: 10–13 hours per 24 hours, including naps
- 6–12 years: 9–12 hours per 24 hours
- 13–18 years: 8–10 hours per 24 hours

EXERCISE CHECKLIST. A check mark in any of these categories suggests that your child may benefit from improved exercise habits. Refer to Chapter 2 to find out how to help your child in this important foundational area of reading success.

❑ My child exercises less than 1 hour per day.

❑ My child's pediatrician has told me that my child needs to get more exercise.

❑ My child's pediatrician has told me that my child is overweight.

❑ My child has trouble paying attention.

Monitoring Your Child's Emotional Well-Being

In addition to the physiological foundations of nutrition, sleep, and exercise that are important for reading success, your child needs a sense of emotional well-being; as I've noted, disturbed emotional states interfere with optimal brain function. A check mark in any of the categories in the Emotional Well-Being Checklist suggests that your child may need extra support managing his feelings. Refer to Chapter 2 to find out about how to help your child in this important foundational area of reading success.

EMOTIONAL WELL-BEING CHECKLIST

❑ My child's pediatrician has told me that my child may need extra support managing her feelings.

❑ My child's teacher has told me that my child may need extra support managing his feelings.

❑ There is a change happening in my child's life or in my child's family life.

❑ There is stress in my child's life or in my child's family life.

❑ There is conflict in my child's life or in my child's family life.

❑ My child seems to worry a lot.

❑ My child seems to cry easily.

❑ My child seems to get angry easily.

❑ My child seems to get frustrated easily.

❑ My child often seems sad.

❑ My child's moods seem very intense.

❑ My child's moods seem to change often and unexpectedly.

❑ My child seems to be having trouble sleeping well, eating well, and/or playing well with other children.

Monitoring Your Child's Behavior

Turning to behaviors, the third foundational area, your child needs a repertoire of on-task behaviors to support reading success. As described in Chapter 2, managing behavior is important because your child needs to be able to sit for an extended period of time and follow directions to achieve reading success. A check mark in any of the categories in the Behavioral Checklist suggests that your child may need extra support managing her behavior. Refer to Chapter 2 to read about how to help your child in this important foundational area.

BEHAVIORAL CHECKLIST

❑ My child's pediatrician, or another medical professional, has told me·that my child needs helps managing her behavior.

❑ My child's teacher, or another educational professional, has told me that my child needs help managing her behavior.

❑ My child has difficulty sitting still for a developmentally appropriate length of time (15 minutes for 5-year-olds, 20 minutes for 6-year-olds, 25 minutes for 7-year-olds, and so on).

❑ My child often has difficulty following directions.

❑ I often experience my child as uncooperative.

❑ I often experience my child as avoidant (for instance, avoiding reading and writing activities).

❑ My child has tantrums.

❑ My child hurts herself and/or others.

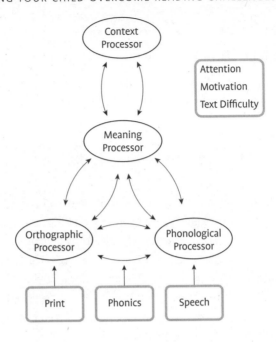

Monitoring Your Child's Visual Processing

Having considered the role that the foundational areas have in supporting reading success, let's now turn to the cognitive aspects that come into play. Children need both accurate eyesight (visual acuity) and accurate visual processing (the brain's ability to interpret visual information) to become successful readers. A check mark in any of the categories in the Visual Processing Checklist suggests that your child may need extra support with visual acuity and/or visual processing. Refer to Chapter 5 to find out about how to help your child in this important area.

VISUAL PROCESSING CHECKLIST

❑ My child's pediatrician, or another health professional, has told me that my child needs help with visual acuity and/or visual processing.

❑ My child's teacher, or another education professional, has told me that my child needs help with visual acuity and/or visual processing.

❑ My child rubs his eyes a lot.

❑ My child is slow to name shapes and letters.

❑ My child has trouble copying letters, shapes, pictures, and/or words.

❑ My child has difficulty matching letters, shapes, pictures, and/or words.

❑ My child has difficulty detecting similarities and differences in letters, shapes, pictures, and/or words.

❑ My child has difficulty remembering what she has viewed, such as sight words.

❑ My child gets easily distracted by things that he sees.

❑ My child often loses her place when she is reading.

❑ My child has difficulty remembering to read from left to right.

Note: If, as a result of completing the Visual Processing checklist, you think that you would like to pursue a professional evaluation of your child's visual processing skills, you can search the Internet using the phrase "Visual processing testing near me."

Monitoring Your Child's Auditory Processing

Your child also needs accurate hearing (auditory acuity) and accurate auditory processing (the brain's ability to interpret auditory information) to achieve reading success. A check mark in any of the categories in the Auditory Processing Checklist suggests that your child may need extra support with hearing and/or auditory processing. Refer to Chapter 6 to find out about how to help your child in this important foundational area.

AUDITORY PROCESSING CHECKLIST

❑ My child's pediatrician, or another health professional, has told me that my child needs help with hearing and/or auditory processing.

❑ My child's teacher, or another education professional, has told me that my child needs help with hearing and/or auditory processing.

❑ My child had multiple ear infections when younger and/or still has frequent ear infections. (Multiple ear infections are a risk factor for hearing and/or auditory processing difficulty.)

❑ My child often asks me to repeat what I have said.

❑ My child has difficulty remembering a list of three items.

❑ My child has difficulty rhyming.

❑ My child has difficulty identifying the first sound in words.

❑ My child has difficulty identifying the final sound in three-letter words.

❑ My child has difficulty identifying the final sound in multisyllable words (for example: What's the last sound in the word *refrigerator?*).

❑ My child has difficulty identifying the middle sound in three-letter words.

❑ My child has difficulty replacing the first sound in a word with a different sound (for example: If the word is *pig* and you replace the *pah* with a *bah*, what word do you have?).

❑ My child has difficulty replacing the last sound in a word with a different sound (for example: If the word is *big* and you replace the *gah* with a *tah*, what word do you have?).

❑ My child has difficulty replacing the middle sound in a word with a different sound (for example: If the word is *big* and you replace the *ih* with an *ah*, what word do you have?).

❑ My child has difficulty listening to a group of four words and figuring out which word doesn't belong (for example: If the words are *goat*, *boat*, *dig*, and *float*, which one doesn't belong? If the words are *big*, *hat*, *boat*, and *bat*, which one doesn't belong? If the words are *fad*, *dip*, *lid*, and *head*, which one doesn't belong?).

Note: If, as a result of completing the Auditory Processing Checklist, you think that you would like to pursue a professional evaluation of your child's hearing and/or auditory processing skills, you can search the Internet using the phrase "Auditory processing testing near me."

Monitoring Your Child's Phonics Ability

Phonics refers to a reader's ability to match print and sound. While accurate print identification is produced by a reader's visual processing system, and accurate sound identification is produced by a reader's auditory processing system, phonics ability enables the reader to match the output of these two systems. The potential causes of a phonics problem are (1) difficulty processing print (which impedes accurate print and sound matching); (2) difficulty processing sound (which impedes accurate print and sound matching); and (3) difficulty with accurate print and sound matching. Your child may have difficulty in one, two, or all three of these areas. Therefore, if your child has difficulty with the following Phonics Skills Checklist, be sure to also use the previous Visual and Auditory Processing Checklists to identify the source(s) of the phonics problem. A check mark in any of these categories suggests that your child may need extra support with phonics. Refer to Chapter 7 to find out how to help your child in this important area of reading. Also, if you have any difficulty using the checklist, see Chapter 7 for additional information on the topic.

PHONICS SKILLS CHECKLIST

❑ My child has difficulty matching the following letters with their matching consonant sounds: *b, c, d, f, g, h, j, k, l, m, n, p, q, r, s, t, v, x, z,* and usually *w* and *y.*

❑ My child has difficulty matching the following letters with their short-vowel sounds: *a, e, i, o, u,* and sometimes *y.*

❑ My child has difficulty matching the following letters with their long-vowel sounds: *a, e, i, o, u,* and sometimes *y.*

❑ My child has difficulty matching the following letter pairs with their consonant blend sounds: *bl, cl, fl, gl, pl, sl, br, cr, dr, fr, gr, pr, tr, wr, sc, sk, sm, sn, sp, st, sw, sch, scr, squ, str, spr, spl, shr, dw, tw,* and *thr.*

❑ My child has difficulty matching the following letter pairs with their consonant digraph sounds: *ch, sh, wh,* and *th.*

❑ My child has difficulty matching the following letter pairs with their diphthong vowel sounds: *ai, ay, ea, ee, oa, oi, oo, ou,* and *oy.*

Monitoring Your Child's Vocabulary Knowledge

In reading, the word *vocabulary* means knowing the meaning of words. When children read, they need to know the meaning of virtually every word to comprehend the meaning of the text. *In my opinion,* **all children** *benefit from activities that expand their vocabularies, and therefore I urge all parents to read Chapter 8 and engage in the recommended vocabulary-expanding activities.* In addition, be sure to refer to Chapter 8 if you check any of the items in the Vocabulary Skills Checklist:

VOCABULARY SKILLS CHECKLIST

❑ I have been told by a medical or educational professional that my child needs to expand her vocabulary.

❑ My child has a learning difference (for example, a diagnosis of autism or specific language disorder).

❑ My child had, or has, frequent ear infections.

❑ My child is growing up learning more than one language (Note: Learning more than one language will ultimately be of great benefit to your child. While she is young, though, be sure to use the activities in Chapter 8 for vocabulary building in both, or all, languages.)

❑ My child tends to be very quiet and not speak very often.

❑ My child started speaking after 2 years of age.

❑ My child has trouble understanding when I read to her and/or when she reads on her own.

Monitoring Your Child's Reading Comprehension and Metacognition

The word *comprehension* means understanding what you are reading, and the word *metacognition* means being aware of your own thinking. Both skills are essential for reading success. *As with the vocabulary interventions I have recommended, I believe that* **all children** *will benefit from the comprehension and metacognitive strengthening activities in this book.* In addition, a check mark in any of the categories in the following Comprehension and Metacognition Checklist suggests that your child may need extra support in these areas. Refer to Chapter 9 to find out how to help your child in these important areas of reading. Also, if you have any difficulty using the checklist, see Chapter 9 for additional information on the topic.

COMPREHENSION AND METACOGNITION CHECKLIST

❑ A professional educator has told me that my child needs help strengthening his listening and/or reading comprehension.

❑ My child seems to have difficulty comprehending when I read to him.

❑ My child seems to have difficulty comprehending when he reads.

❑ When reading a story, my child has difficulty identifying the setting.

❑ When reading a story, my child has difficulty identifying the main character or characters.

❑ When reading a story, my child has difficulty identifying the main character's problem.

❑ When reading a story, my child has difficulty identifying the plot.

❏ When reading a story, my child has difficulty identifying the outcome.

❏ When reading a story or informational text, my child has difficulty making inferences.

❏ When reading a story or informational text, my child has difficulty recalling the sequence of events.

❏ When reading informational text, my child has difficulty differentiating between explanatory, comparison–contrast, problem–solution, and cause–effect text structures.

❏ Before reading, my child forgets to preview the text.

❏ Before reading, my child forgets to activate his prior knowledge.

❏ Before reading, my child forgets to set a purpose for reading.

❏ Before and during reading, my child forgets to make text predictions.

❏ Before, during, and after reading, my child forgets to visualize what she has read.

❏ My child has difficulty summarizing what she has read.

❏ My child has difficulty knowing what to do if she hasn't understood what she has read.

Monitoring Your Child's Reading Level

One of the most important factors to help your child overcome reading difficulty is to provide him with books that are at his correct reading level. Books that are too difficult for your child interfere with his ability to comprehend what he is reading, increase his anxiety about reading, lower his self-esteem, and reduce his motivation to read. In contrast, books that are too easy will not provide enough challenge to promote skill growth.

The easiest way to determine the optimal text level to use with your child is to ask your child's teacher to provide you with this information. If this option is not possible for you, or if you feel that the information that you are getting from your child's teacher may not be accurate, you can determine your child's reading level yourself.

To determine your child's reading level, you will need to have him read texts to you that are at different levels of difficulty and then observe how well he reads each one. Here are two methods to help you find your child's reading level. Once you know your child's reading level, continue to provide him with texts at that level for reading practice until the texts begin to seem too easy.

Reading-Level Guidelines

1. Select a book that is *2 years below your child's grade level* (the grade at which your child is enrolled in school). Count out the first 100 words of the book and then have your child read that block of text to you. Track the number of reading errors that your child makes when reading the first 100 words. If your child makes more than five errors in the first 100 words, the book is too difficult. Repeat the process with a book that is one grade year lower in difficulty. If your child makes three-to-five errors, texts at this difficulty level are ideal for reading with your child. If your child makes two or fewer reading errors in the first 100 words, the book may be too easy for your child. In this case, select a book one grade level higher.

2. Open a free account at the website Newsela.com. Click on the tab "Text Level," and then select the text level that is *2 years below your child's grade level*. Have your child read you the text. If your child can read approximately 97% of the words in the text correctly, the text level is good for practicing reading with you. If the text seems too easy for your child, proceed to the next higher-level text. If your child is reading with less than 95% accuracy, proceed to the next lower-level text. Once you identify the text level at which your child is reading with approximately 97% accuracy, continue to use texts at this level of difficulty. In addition, you can click on "Activities" and then the "Quiz" tabs to check your child's comprehension of what he is reading. Continue to use the leveled texts provided on the website such that your child reads with approximately 97% accuracy and good comprehension when reading with you.

Monitoring Your Child's Attention during Reading

Attention is the ability to concentrate on the task at hand, and is necessary for successful reading to occur. Attention problems have multiple causes. Use the following Attention Checklist to determine whether your child might be having difficulty in this area. A check mark in any of these categories suggests that your child may need extra help strengthening her attention. If needed, refer to Chapter 10 to find out how to help your child in this important area of reading.

ATTENTION CHECKLIST

❑ My child does not have a dedicated physical space for reading.

❑ My child does not have a routine time each day when she practices reading.

❑ There are a lot of distractions, such as noise and activity, in my child's home.

❑ My child has a distraction-free place in which to work but still has trouble concentrating on her reading.

❑ My child seems easily distracted when he is reading.

❑ My child tries to pay attention when she is reading but still has trouble understanding what she has read.

Monitoring Your Child's Motivation to Read

In general motivation refers to a person's desire, or willingness, to participate in a particular activity. When educators discuss children's motivation to read, they think about how interested the child is in reading, how dedicated the child is to improving her reading ability, and how much confidence the child has in her ability to read and to grow as a reader. Motivation is central to reading achievement because motivated readers read much more than unmotivated readers. Use the following Motivation Checklist to determine whether your child might be having difficulty with reading motivation. A check mark in any of the categories suggests that your child may need extra help in this area. If so, refer to Chapter 10 to find out how to help your child in this area.

MOTIVATION CHECKLIST

❏ My child does not usually pick reading as an activity of choice.

❏ When I tell my child that it is time to read, he resists participating.

❏ When my child is reading, he typically wants to stop.

❏ When my child is asked to describe how he feels about reading, he uses negative words such as *hard* and *boring*. He may also say that he hates reading.

What Should I Do If My Child Is Having Difficulty with More Than One Area?

Rest assured that, if your child is having difficulty in more than one of the areas that have been discussed, she is very much like a great many other children who experience difficulty in multiple areas related to reading success. The trick to minimizing these difficulties is to know which areas your child struggles with and to provide targeted intervention and support directly in these areas. The remainder of this book is devoted exactly to this goal.

When Should I Contact a Professional for Help?

The main purpose of this book is to provide you as parents with a substantive amount of information about what needs to happen for your child to be a successful reader and how to help your child overcome reading difficulty. While I am a firm believer that parents are capable of greatly enhancing their child's ability to read, I also believe that there are times when professional evaluations and interventions are called for. My suggestion is to first read and use this book to the best of your ability. If, after several months of consistent effort, you are not seeing noticeable reading improvement in your child, or if a professional at your child's school is advocating for an immediate professional evaluation of your child, then by all means follow this advice. And if you have the gut feeling that something is terribly wrong, find out how to consult a professional on your own. The information, resources, and activities in this book are designed to inform and help you and your child. However, if additional support services are also needed, don't hesitate to seek them out. See the box on pages 55–56 for sage advice from one mother who went through this process to help her son.

Chapter Highlights

Becoming a successful reader can be a complicated process, and many factors need to be considered when a child is experiencing reading difficulty. Using checklists, this chapter provides guidance regarding how to determine whether your child is having difficulty in one or more of the areas that contribute to reading success. After one or more problem areas have been identified, parents are then guided to a specific subsequent chapter or chapters to learn more about the topic and how to help their child remediate the difficulty.

Advice from a Parent on Advocating for a Child Who Is Struggling with Reading

Where to start?

My son was a very early talker with an amazing vocabulary—very vocal, very bright. But I noticed very early that he seemed to have attention issues but . . . he was a boy, right?

In kindergarten, he did well, but the school he was at didn't give any direct phonics instruction. He was able to read, but his writing was illegible at times. His letter formation was incorrect, and letters looked like numbers (n and 6, e and s). At times when he was writing, he would ask me "What does that letter look like again?" He was aware of his difficulties at such a young age, but his writing—that was the first alarm. His letter and number confusion and reversals continued into third grade. It was very hard for him to write words that he could read, and he spelled them differently each time he would write them. Sometimes "because" was "becuz," and at other times it was "becawse"—on the same page. That was a red flag for me. Then I noticed that he couldn't read multisyllable words. He would just mumble something when he got to them. Once he told me that the words were moving on the page. I'll never forget that.

I knew something was wrong. My son is so smart; he could memorize and compensate, but he couldn't decode. I remember that he would push his fists against each other so hard that his face would turn red. He would scream that he was stupid. I couldn't let that keep happening. As a mom, that was my breaking point.

Then things got really difficult. The school tested him, and he passed all the universal tests, so I had to continue to fight with them to get him tested. One year I had to bring an advocate to the meetings with me. Finally, in third grade, he qualified for extra services.

Here are some tips I have for parents of struggling readers:

- *Keep everything, save everything, date everything. That's key. I kept all of my son's notebooks, writing, and schoolwork. I would bring them to meetings with me.*

- *Get an advocate. If the school is refusing your child extra support services and you feel that he needs them, hire a professional to advocate on your behalf.*

- *Reach out to your child's teachers. Sometimes, we think that* teachers don't want to be bothered. I found just the opposite. My son's teachers were happy to hear from me and were great about providing me with ideas and materials for helping my son.

- Videotape your child at home. Sometimes his teachers would say things like "That doesn't happen here" or "He doesn't do that in school." I used my phone as a video camera to capture how upset and frustrated my son would get with his work at home. Then the teachers could see what was happening when he wasn't at school.

Get informed about the services your school district offers and how to qualify for them. Find out what extra support services your school district offers and the criteria for receiving those services. You have to find out how to get the golden ticket [of extra support services] for your child.

—Mrs. S., on helping her struggling reader

5

What Should I Do If My Child Is Having Difficulty with Visual Processing?

I believe that life is a process of continuous change and a constant struggle to make that change one for the better.

—LEE KUAN YEW (overcame reading difficulty to become the first prime minister of Singapore)

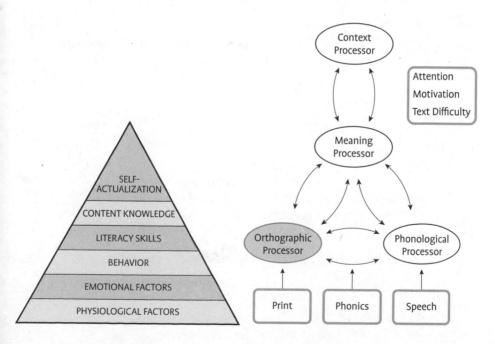

This chapter can help you and your child if:

❑ A professional has told you that your child has visual processing difficulty.

❑ You've used the Visual Processing Checklist in Chapter 4 to determine that your child has visual processing difficulty.

❑ Or you're seeing signs that might point to a visual processing difficulty, such as:

- Your child squints when reading.

- Your child holds reading material very close to her face.

- Your child has trouble distinguishing shapes accurately in printed material.

In this chapter I will:

1. Help you understand how print is effectively processed during reading.

2. Review the likely culprits that interfere with efficient print processing.

3. Provide you with activities and resources that can help you to help your child strengthen his visual processing system.

Before you get started on this chapter . . .

Check off all of the following items to make sure that your child's brain is optimally prepared for visual processing. *If you can't say "yes" to any item, refer back to Chapter 2.*

❑ My child usually eats a diet high in fruits and vegetables and low in processed foods (food packaged in a box or bag that has more than one ingredient).

❑ My child usually gets 8–10 hours of sleep per night.

❑ My child usually gets 1 hour of vigorous physical activity per day.

❑ My child is able to feel, talk about, and appropriately manage a wide range of emotions.

❑ My child's behavior usually seems focused and on task.

How Does the Brain Learn to Read Letters?

The visual processing of print takes place in both the eyes and the brain. Briefly, the centers of our retinas, the foveae, take in print and transmit it to a small section of the visual processing system located on the left side of the brain known as "the brain's letterbox" (*Reading in the Brain: The New Science of How We Read,* Dehaene, 2009, p. 53). Through brain imaging, researchers have been able to determine that everyone who reads, regardless of the language in which he is reading, transmits print in the same way: from the fovea to the brain's letterbox.

> " *I took my son for vision therapy, and it really helped."*
> —Julie Franklin, mother of a formerly struggling reader

The brain's letterbox itself is developed within a neural system called *connectionism* (*Overcoming Dyslexia: A New and Complete Science-Based Program for Reading Problems at Any Level,* Shaywitz, 2004), in which the more often stimuli are perceived together, the stronger and faster their connections become. The brain uses connectionism in learning to identify letters. For example, when learning the capital letter *L*, the brain sees the pairing of a single vertical line, |, and a single horizontal line, __. Eventually these two images will be connected in the reader's mind into the capital letter *L*. The more often that the brain simultaneously sees the pairing of these two images, the stronger and faster the identification of the letter *L* becomes. The same process take places for all capital and lowercase letters. The more often that the reader sees the paired graphic images (the lines and curves that create specific letters), the faster and stronger the recognition of these letters becomes.

How Does the Brain Learn to Read Words?

The neural system of connectionism also underlies how our brain learns to read words. It does so by connecting the common patterns of letters within words. The system of letter recognition that organizes the patterning of letters that form words in the brain is called the interletter associational unit system (*Overcoming Dyslexia*, Shaywitz, 2004), which was introduced in Chapter 3. Despite its long name, this system is easy to understand if you think about how your smartphone works. On your phone, if you type in the letters *Li*, your phone generates the word *Like*. Similarly, if you type in the letters *Lo*, your phone generates the word *Love*. The letterbox in your brain works in the same way. Based on connectionism, and like your smartphone, the brain generates letters that are likely to follow the target letters. For example, after the letterbox identifies the letter *L* it generates letters that are likely to follow it: *a, e, i, o,* and *u*. At the same time, the letterbox (and your smartphone) suppresses letters that are unlikely to follow, such as *l, b, d, f, g*. The more often our brain sees specific letters sequenced together, the more quickly and easily it recognizes that sequence as a word. It is this system of likely letter activation and suppression, based on neural connectionism, that allows skilled readers to easily and quickly process sequences of letters into formed words.

> *"I found that having my son read on the computer and enlarging the font size for him really helped."*
> —Roselind Frontenac, mother of a struggling reader

Keep in mind however that in the human brain the letter activation and suppression system is dependent on instantaneous letter recognition. If it takes a reader too long to recognize any individual letter, the entire system of activating letters that are likely to follow a target letter, and suppressing letters that are unlikely to follow a target letter, will not be engaged. If this happens, you will notice that your child is reading "letter by letter." I more fully explain how to address this important aspect of visual processing in the sections that follow.

Why Is My Child Having Visual Processing Difficulty?

Print processing difficulty can occur at the three levels described earlier: (1) in the eye where print is initially perceived, (2) in brain's letterbox where letters are identified, and (3) in the brain's letterbox where letter sequences become recognized as words. The recommendations, activities, and resources I offer can help you address the likely causes of visual processing difficulty.

Addressing Visual Processing Difficulty

The Importance of an Eye Examination

Since visual processing of print starts in the eye, it is essential that a child who is having any difficulty at all processing print have a thorough eye examination. A reader must be able to see print clearly to quickly and efficiently process it. Hints that your child may be having vision problems include squinting when reading, moving the text closer and farther away during reading to try to make the print clearer, and/or losing track of where she is on the page. Be sure to get your child a thorough eye examination if you suspect any problem at all in the area of visual processing.

The Importance of Speed of Letter Recognition

After a vision problem has been ruled out or corrected by an eye care professional, the next step to strengthening your child's visual processing is to help him with speed of letter recognition. It is not enough for your child to be able to correctly name letters; to be able to read well, your child must be able to name letters *instantaneously*. Again, the reason for this is that if your child's letter name recognition is not instantaneous, the entire interletter associational unit system will not be activated, and you will find your child reading letter by letter. So, let's get started with some activities, books, and online resources that you can use to help your child achieve automatic letter recognition.

Speed of Letter Recognition Activities

Although there are only 26 letters in the English alphabet, due to our print system of uppercase and lowercase letters, children actually need to learn to instantaneously identify 52 letters (26 uppercase and 26 lowercase letters). I strongly suggest helping your child master the 26 uppercase (capital) letters first. According to reading researcher Elizabeth Sulzby, developmentally, children learn to print capital letters first. Therefore, reading capital letters first also tends to be easiest for them. After mastering the 26 capital letters, help your child master the 26 lowercase letters.

One approach to increasing your child's speed of letter recognition skill is to work with *multisensory materials*. Multisensory materials are those that use all of your child's senses (seeing, touching, moving, tasting, smelling, and hearing) to enhance learning. Some multisensory materials that children enjoy using to enhance speed of letter recognition include shaving cream, pudding (before it sets), finger paint, and sand. These materials can be used on waxed paper, paper trays, or aluminum pans to practice letter shapes. Children also enjoy making letters with playdough, clay, pipe cleaners, and letter stamps. Letters that are already made of plastic, wood, sponges, and sandpaper are also considered multisensory and can be used for art activities, bath time, and matching games.

In addition to practicing letters with multisensory materials, speed of letter recognition can be strengthened with rote practice and a stopwatch. For this activity, create random strings of letters, beginning with capital letters, for your child to read. Then, time your child reading the letter strings using either a traditional stopwatch or the stopwatch feature on your smartphone. Help your child keep track of how quickly she can correctly read the letter strings.

Another enjoyable way to work on speed of letter recognition is by playing a letter memory board game, in which participants match pairs of letters. The game can be played in three ways: (1) matching pairs of uppercase letters, (2) matching pairs of lowercase letters, and (3) matching uppercase and lowercase letter pairs.

Books that strengthen children's knowledge of letter names also strengthen their speed of letter recognition skill. Here are a few that I personally recommend:

✦ *Eating the Alphabet: Fruits and Vegetables from A to Z* (Lois Ehlert, 1989). This text provides boldly colorful illustrations and accompanying names of fruits and vegetables for all the letters of the alphabet. Not only will your child improve her speed of letter recognition, but her vocabulary and nutrition knowledge will grow as well. This is a great book to keep in the kitchen, to use to construct a shopping list, or even to take to the grocery store with you.

✦ *LMNOPea-quel* (Keith Baker, 2017). This delicately illustrated rhyming alphabet book features professions for each letter, starting with architects, authors, actors, and botanists. With this book, your child will strengthen his letter name knowledge and also vastly expand his vocabulary for, and knowledge of, career choices.

✦ *D is for Dump Truck: A Construction Alphabet* (Michael Shoulders, 2016). Does your child love the world of construction? If so, this is the book for your family. B is for bulldozer, D is for dump truck, F is for front-end loader! Come strengthen your child's speed of letter recognition, while helping her read the names of favorite construction vehicles and tools.

✦ *ABC Dream* (Kim Krans, 2013). For a quieter time, try *ABC Dream*. This book is filled with intriguing pen and ink drawings, highlighted with watercolors. Each page contains a different letter and pictures of animals and objects that start with that letter. Enjoy a work of art and strengthen letter recognition at the same time.

✦ *Race from A to Z* (Jon Scieszka, 2014). For a fun time, try this book, which features animated vehicles (Monster Truck Max, Hook and Ladder Lucy, and Tow Truck Ted) all racing from A to Z.

In addition to sharing books with their parents, most children enjoy using iPads and laptop computers. Below are five websites that I highly recommend for strengthening children's letter recognition skills.

✦ ABCYa.com. This website provides free, educational games for children ages PreK through 6. In addition to being able to select the difficulty level of the material for your child, you can choose the topic on which you want him to focus. Letter identification activities include Alphabet Bingo, KPK Talk to Me Alphabet, Alphabetical Order, and Alphabet Bubble.

✦ Starfall.com. This website offers some free online learning activities for children in kindergarten through third grade and additional access to a wider range of educational resources with a low-cost subscription. Many school districts buy subscriptions to this website, indicating its value in educators' eyes.

✦ Literactive.com. This is another free literacy education website; however, registration is required. Many categories of learning activities can be accessed at this website. Activities that enhance the speed of letter recognition include Alphabet Awareness, Alphabet Order, Match Capitals, and Match Smalls.

✦ Mrsjonesroom.com. This website is created by a classroom teacher who shares free online activities that she uses with her students. Just click any letter to see a list of activities, songs, and poems that you can complete with your child.

✦ FunbrainJr.com. This website and computer app extend the famous Funbrain games to serve an audience of younger children. Follow the links to "Letter Splash" to find fun games such as Beaker Bonanza, Puzzle Me, Skater Sequence, and Trading Spaces.

In addition to resources that directly strengthen letter naming speed, your child's speed of letter recognition can be enhanced by using resources that facilitate general visual processing skill:

✦ Ourjourneywestward.com is a website that provides "brain training" activities for visual attention and visual processing.

✦ EyeCanLearn.com is a website devoted to strengthening generalized visual discrimination skills.

✦ Tangoes is a puzzle game in which children use puzzle shapes (tangrams) to recreate picture card images (available online at Amazon).

✦ *Where's Waldo?* (Handford, 1987) is a famous and fun book that parents and children can enjoy together. Here children search to find the cartoon character, Waldo, in a variety of playful and interesting settings.

Word Families/Phonograms

In addition to helping children achieve instantaneous letter recognition skills, efficient visual processing is greatly enhanced by the practice of *word families*. Word families are commonly found letter patterns in the English language. For example, *ab*, *an*, and *at* are three common word families. In the literacy world, the technical word for word families is *phonograms*. Practicing the reading of word family words is an optimal route to strengthening visual processing because word family words strengthen the brain's interletter associational unit system. Stated differently, every time a word family word is read, that pattern of letters is strengthened as a unit within the brain's letterbox.

The book *The New Reading Teacher's Book of Lists* (Fry, Fountoukidis, & Polk, 1985) lists the 88 major phonogram families and the 126 minor phonogram families (see the Appendix for lists of these word families). The book also lists all the words that fall into each family. So, for example, the book shows that the *ab* family contains the words *cab*, *gab*, *jab*, *tab*, *crab*, *drab*, *grab*, *scab*, *slab*, and *stab*. Similarly, the book shows that the *ace* family contains the words *face*, *lace*, *mace*, *pace*, *race*, *brace*, *grace*, *place*, *space*, and *trace*. *In my opinion, helping your child master all of the words in the major and minor word families is one of the single most important things that you can do to help your child become a strong reader.*

How to Approach the Study of Word Families

As in studying individual letters, word families should be studied and mastered in an incremental manner. What I mean by this is, if you are using the lists in the Appendix, begin with the first family (*ab*) in the major phonogram list. Once your child can read all of the words in the *ab* family quickly and easily, proceed to the next family (*ace*) in the major phonogram list. However, be sure that when your child is studying the *ace* family, you continue to practice the *ab* group. Likewise, when both of these families are mastered, and you add the third phonogram (*ack*), continue to practice the already mastered families. Proceeding in this manner will help your child incrementally learn all the words in the major and minor phonogram families, while simultaneously strengthening the interletter associational unit system responsible for efficient print processing.

Many different activities can be used to study word families. A simple do-it-yourself activity can be made with index cards. Mark one index card with the phonogram itself (let's say *ab*) and the other index cards with the starting letters needed to make words in that family. So, for example, for the *ab* word family, create index cards marked *c, g, j, t, cr, dr, gr, sc, sl,* and *st.* Then have your child practice making words by attaching the starting letters to each letter pattern.

Word family activities can also be purchased. A great resource for buying these activities is Lakeshore Learning, a company that creates and sells high-quality educational materials. Three great purchases to strengthen word family knowledge are Word Building Blocks, Word Family Flip Books, and Word Family Practice Cards. In the Word Building Blocks activity, letter blocks snap together to make word families, and then children add initial letters to make words from that family. The Word Family Flip Book package contains 30 flip books, each featuring a different word family. Children turn the pages to create new words in that family. The Word Family Practice Cards provide 40 write and wipe practice cards. Each card features a different family. Children add initial letters to make words from that family.

In addition to using hands-on word family activities, reading books to your child that emphasize word family knowledge is very useful. Four classics are *The Cat in the Hat* (1957); *One Fish, Two Fish* (1960); *Green Eggs and Ham* (1960); and *Hop on Pop* (1963)—all by Dr. Seuss.

As with strengthening the speed of letter recognition, word family knowledge can also be facilitated using online activities. Here are three websites that I like for attaining this goal.

✦ TurtleDiary.com. This website provides educational games for children, with some resources available for free and others available for a nominal fee. To locate Word Family Games, click on "Games," then "Language Games," and last "Word Families." The website will take you to links for a wide selection of word families. Click on any family to see all the words in that family and a section of games to improve knowledge of that family.

✦ ReadWriteThink.org. Created by the International Literacy Association, the world's largest professional literacy association, this website is completely free. Its purpose is to provide high-quality learning resources to educators and parents. The website offers a variety of activities for practicing word families, but one that I particularly like is called Word Family Sort (click on "Student Interactives" under "Classroom Resources"). In this activity, children are presented with words and need to sort them into their current word families.

✦ Enchantedlearning.com. This website for parents and teachers provides both free and low-cost educational resources. Parents can access free lists of word families and corresponding words for each family. In addition, activities for practicing word families can be accessed.

Sight Words

In addition to mastering instantaneous letter recognition and word families, children need to master sight words to be proficient at visual processing. Sight words are words that educators believe students need to be able to recognize instantaneously. There are two subcategories of sight words: high-frequency sight words and thematic sight words.

High-Frequency Sight Words

High-frequency sight words are words that occur very often in the English language. A few examples are *the, this, these,* and *those.* It is critical that children be able to read these words instantaneously because they are so often seen in printed text. High-frequency words are also often phonetically irregular, meaning they are very difficult to sound out. Therefore, children need to read them "by sight," and these sight words are taught using activities and techniques that are different from those used to teach words from phonetically consistent word families.

When thinking about activities to teach high-frequency sight words, my mind immediately goes back to *The New Reading Teacher's Book of Lists.* In addition to listing all of the words in the major and minor phonogram families, this book lists the 1,000 most-frequent sight words in the English language, in order of frequency (see the Appendix for the list of these words). For example, the first list of 25 words starts with the word *the* because *the* is the most common word in the English language. To read directly from the lists, begin with the first list and practice this one until your child easily and quickly achieves 100% mastery. Then proceed to the next list. While working on the second list, be sure to continue to practice the first list. Similarly, when working on the third list, be sure to continue to practice the first two lists, and so on.

In addition to practicing the lists of high-frequency sight words, there are activities that you can create and/or purchase to help your child learn these extremely important words. For a do-it-yourself activity or game, you can use index cards to make flash cards of the words on the list. If you make two index cards for each word, you can use these to play

"The challenge of teaching your struggling reader may seem like an impossible undertaking. But with time and patience, the results will amaze you. Your child's teacher is a resource—she plants the seeds—but it is up to you to give your flower water and sunlight. A very common tool is the use of sight words. Frequently used words—from speech and text—can be written on index cards and practiced on a daily basis. This should be practiced at least once a day. Once a word is mastered, place a star or sticker on the card as a visual cue to increase confidence. Then take the conceptual idea of words and give them concrete meaning. Label the world around them. Use index cards to fill your home with labels to provide reading opportunities. Teach your children that everything around them is a word. Although this new home decorating may not be your favorite style, remember that this is only temporary, and you have a long-term goal in mind. Point out text as often as possible: from labels, on signs, on television, at the grocery store, and so on. A flower does not grow overnight, but if you create the right setting, you will watch it blossom."

—Jessica Vitali, teacher of English

The Memory Game, in which all cards are placed face down, and players take turns finding cards that match. If you prefer to purchase activity materials, Lakeshore Learning offers a Fishing for Sight Words game in which children practice catching sight word fish with a magnetic fishing pole. Another popular and fun choice from this company is Sight-Word Bingo. Write and Wipe Sight-Words Practice Cards, also available from Lakeshore, are additional, valuable practice materials.

If you and your child prefer online activities, you can search for "How to Teach Sight Words" on themeasuredmom.com website. ABCYa .com has two online sight word activities: Out of Sight Words, and Sight Word BINGO. Crawfordthecat.com has a 100-sight-word online search game. Turtlediary.com has four online sight word games: Complete the Sentence with the Correct Sight Word, Spell the Sight Words, Choose the Correct Sight Word, and Make Pairs of Sight Words.

Thematic Sight Words

Thematic sight words are words associated with any specialized topic. For example, the topic *dinosaurs* is associated with the thematic words *Tyrannosaurus Rex, Brachiosaurus, Diplodocus, Brontosaurus,* and *Stegosaurus.* What is amazing about thematic words is that, even when they are long and complicated like these dinosaur words are, struggling readers can often read them quickly and easily because they often find these words interesting and because they are derived from a relatively closed group of word options.

An ideal way to practice reading thematic words with your child is to find a topic in which she is especially interested. Some favorite thematic topics are particular sports (soccer, baseball, football, tennis, surfing, fishing, skateboarding, dancing, skiing, skating) and/or sports figures, pop culture, music and/or musicians, the environment, cooking, history, self-care, careers, and travel. After you and your child have selected a topic of interest, do some research to generate a list of words associated with that topic, as in the dinosaur example I just gave. In addition, search for books, games, and websites related to your child's special interest area(s). Your child will readily and easily read and learn words associated with topics that she is motivated to learn about.

Chapter Highlights

The reading process begins with the processing of print. Automatic letter recognition is central to this process, and speed of letter recognition is critical for efficient letter processing. In addition to individual letter recognition, print is processed via word family (phonogram) recognition and through sight words. There are two kinds of sight words: high-frequency sight words and thematic sight words. Letter, word family, and sight word knowledge can all be strengthened by using the activities and resources described in this chapter. The underlying foundations of sleep, nutrition, exercise, emotion, and behaviors all affect the processing of print and should be taken into consideration when assessing and developing a child's print processing. Also, be sure to have your child's eyesight checked by an eye-care specialist if you are at all concerned about his visual processing.

6

What Should I Do If My Child Is Having Difficulty with Auditory Processing?

Do not be embarrassed by your failures; learn from them and start again. Hard-won things are more valuable than those that come too easily.

—RICHARD BRANSON (overcame reading difficulty to become a self-made entrepreneur and billionaire)

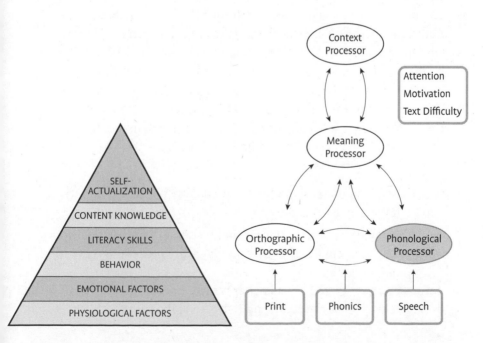

This chapter can help you and your child if:

❑ A professional has told you that your child has auditory processing difficulty.

❑ You've used the Auditory Processing Checklist in Chapter 4 to determine that your child has auditory processing difficulty.

❑ You're seeing signs that might point to an auditory processing difficulty, such as:

- Your child often says "What?" or asks you to repeat what you're reading aloud.

- Your child seems to need the TV or other device at a higher volume than the rest of your family.

- Your child seems to misinterpret oral instructions from you on a regular basis.

If you are noticing any of these signs in your child, you're far from alone. *Auditory processing problems are the most common cause of reading difficulty.* So if your child is having trouble reading, you may very well need to use the information in this chapter. Auditory processing difficulty is particularly common in children who have had many ear infections in early childhood because fluid buildup in the ear prevents the brain from clearly differentiating incoming sounds. Prolonged or frequent ear infections impede the development of the auditory processing system, which manages the brain's ability to clearly hear, differentiate, and manipulate sounds. Don't worry; you'll find help in this chapter.

In this chapter I will:

1. Help you understand the term *auditory processing* and its importance to reading.

2. Provide you with activities and resources that can help you help your child strengthen her auditory processing system.

Before you get started on this chapter . . .
Check off all of the following items to make sure that your

child's brain is optimally prepared for auditory processing. *If you can't say "yes" to any item, refer back to Chapter 2.*

- ❑ My child usually eats a diet high in fruits and vegetables, and low in processed foods (food packaged in a box or bag that contains more than one ingredient).
- ❑ My child usually gets 8–10 hours of sleep per night.
- ❑ My child usually gets 1 hour of vigorous physical activity per day.
- ❑ My child is able to feel, talk about, and appropriately manage a wide range of emotions.
- ❑ My child's behavior usually seems focused and on task.

✦ ✦ ✦

What Is Auditory Processing?

The term *auditory processing* refers to the way sounds are processed in the brain. Auditory processing is *not* the same as hearing. Your child may have perfectly normal hearing, but still have difficulty with processing sounds. To understand this difference, think about listening to a song when you can't understand the lyrics; you can hear the song perfectly, but you can't exactly decipher what the singer is saying. This difficulty is what a child with auditory processing experiences all the time; the child can tell that something is being said but cannot decipher what the exact words are. In other words, the child's ear is adequately taking in sounds, but the child's brain needs additional training to help it decipher the exact sounds, and sequence of the sounds, that he is hearing.

How Important Is Auditory Processing to Reading?

Auditory processing is central to reading because reading is largely based on the process of matching print and sounds. A reader who is having difficulty perceiving specific sounds will not be able to successfully navigate this process.

How Can I Help My Child Overcome Auditory Processing Difficulty?

If you suspect any problem at all related to your child's auditory processing system, the first step is to have your child evaluated by a hearing specialist to rule out any hearing problems. Once a professional has determined that your child's hearing is within the normal range, you can proceed with the auditory processing strengthening activities below. While auditory processing difficulty is very common among children with reading challenges, the good news is that it is usually very receptive to remediation. In other words, once a hearing problem has been ruled out, there is a very high likelihood that you can help strengthen your child's auditory processing skills by practicing the activities in this chapter.

> *"If your child is musical or likes to sing, try using karaoke to teach reading. Musical kids process the written word so much better when music is involved. That is how my child started to read with confidence!"*
> —Laura Better-Henry, mother of a formerly struggling reader

To begin, it is important to know a few terms that educators and reading researchers use. *Phonological awareness* refers to the ability to hear segments of sounds within the English language. These segments include words within sentences, syllables within words, and individual sounds within words, including beginning sounds, ending sounds, and middle sounds.

✦ A *rhyme* is two words that end with the same sound. Rhyming words may or may not be derived from the same word family (see Chapter 5 for an introduction to word families). For example, *bat* and *cat* rhyme and are derived from the same word family. In contrast, *late* and *bait* also rhyme but belong to different word families. Whether or not words rhyme depends on how the words *sound*, not on how they are written.

✦ A *phoneme* is the technical word for an individual sound. For example, the word *bat* has three individual sounds: *b*, *a*, and *t*. Individual sounds are the smallest, and therefore the most abstract and hardest to decipher units of sounds in our language. It's much easier for a child to hear a word in a sentence than a single sound in a word.

✦ *Phonemic awareness* is a subcategory of phonological awareness. Phonemic awareness refers to an individual's ability to hear and manipulate individual sounds within words.

When getting ready to help your child strengthen her auditory processing skills, it's important to remember to focus solely on her listening system, and not include tasks and activities that also include visual processing. The focus of auditory processing activities should remain on helping your child strengthen her ability to hear words within sentences, words that rhyme, syllables, and individual sounds.

Remember too that when getting ready to strengthen your child's auditory processing it's best to move from the easiest unit of sounds to perceive (words within sentences) to the most difficult unit of sounds to perceive (individual phonemes). Auditory processing is like any other skill: it is best taught from easiest to most difficult. I've organized the following activities for strengthening your child's auditory skills in this manner—from easiest to hardest. Be sure that your child can easily and quickly complete all of the easier activities before progressing to the more difficult ones.

"My son really had trouble with listening when he was younger. To help him, I started to tell him bedtime stories at night, with the lights out. I tell him stories about my own childhood and about his grandparents', aunts', and uncles' lives. I also tell him stories about when he was a baby, toddler, and young child. He loves these stories and often asks for the same ones over and over again. He's older now, but we still do this because we both love it. He's doing fine with both listening and reading now."

—Laila Robinson, mother of a formerly struggling reader

Strengthening Your Child's Ability to Perceive Words within Sentences

As adults, we often take it for granted that our children understand that spoken language consists of individual words. However, this understanding actually takes several years for children to acquire. In fact, most children don't fully understand the concept of a *word* until they start to receive reading instruction. For most young children, and for many children with reading difficulties, spoken language is perceived as a long, continuous string of sounds rather than as a string of separate words. Therefore, the best starting point for helping your child strengthen his auditory processing system is to practice counting words within spoken sentences. *As a reminder, these activities are just for listening; printed materials should not be used when implementing these suggestions.*

Listening for the Number of Words in a Sentence

How Many Words in a Sentence? is an auditory processing activity that can be played whenever you and your child have some free time, such as when riding in a car, standing in a checkout line at the grocery store, or waiting in a doctor's office. Begin with three-word sentences. For example, you can say, "Let's play How Many Words in a Sentence? Here is the first sentence: 'I like football.' How many words are in that sentence?" Then proceed with similar examples, "I like baseball," "I like soccer," "I like dancing," "I like cooking," and so on. Once your child quickly and easily succeeds in identifying three words in each of these sentences, try a different three-word sentence pattern, such as "Football is fun," "Soccer is fun," and "Dancing is fun." After your child exhibits mastery of counting words within the same pattern of three-word sentence, begin to vary the three-word sentence patterns. For example, "How many words are in the sentence 'George is athletic'? How about in the sentence 'Grandma went shopping'? How about in the sentence 'Monkeys can jump'?" Continue to offer your child a variety of three-word sentences until you're sure she can easily, quickly, and accurately identify three words in three-word sentences.

Once three-word sentences have been mastered, move on to

four-word sentences. As with three-word sentences, start with a single four-word sentence pattern. For example, say, "How many words are in the sentence 'I like playing cards?' "How about in the sentence 'I like building Legos'? What about 'I like baking cookies'?" After your child has mastered the first four-word sentence pattern, switch to another four-word sentence pattern, such as "Nadine is very tall, "Raheem is very smart, "and "Henry is very old." As with the three-word sentences, after four-word sentence patterns have been mastered, continue with a variety of four-word sentences. These may include: "Please pass the coffee." "Can I come too?" "How much is that?" "Can you hurry up?" Last, continue as I've suggested with five-word, six-word, and seven-word sentences. Be sure to vary one-, two-, and three-syllable words as you practice listening for words within sentences.

Going on a Picnic

Going on a Picnic is another auditory processing game for strengthening alphabet knowledge that you and your child can play whenever you have some free time together. The game goes like this: The first player says, "I'm going on a picnic, and I'm bringing apples" (or any item that starts with the letter *a*). The second player then says, "I'm going on a picnic, and I'm bringing apples and bananas" (or any item that starts with *b*). The next person adds, "I'm going on a picnic, and I'm bringing apples, bananas, and cantaloupe" (or any item that starts with *c*). The game continues until one or more players have forgotten a named item. The winner is the last player to remember all of the previously named foods. This game strengthens auditory processing by highlighting individual words within sentences. It also strengthens a child's attention to listening.

Sing!

The idea of singing with your child may be old-fashioned, but it's a time-tested way of strengthening auditory processing. An added benefit of singing together is the emotional bonding that often takes place when people share music. For this activity, I recommend printing a copy of song lyrics for yourself. If your child has one or more favorite music groups, build on her interest by selecting songs from those groups. Once you're familiar with the lyrics, play the songs and sing along together, prompting your child with the lyrics as needed. Again, listening closely to the words within songs will strengthen your child's auditory processing in much the same way as listening closely to words within spoken sentences.

Strengthening Your Child's Ability to Perceive and Generate Rhymes

As explained earlier, *a rhyme* is two words that end with the same sound. Rhyming words may be derived from the same word family (for example, *bat* and *cat*) or from different word families (for example, *late* and *bait*). Whether or not words rhyme depends on how the words *sound*, not on how they are written. Remember, the activities we'll use are just for listening!

> *"Enjoy a good nursery rhyme with your child! Nursery rhymes can help a child who is having reading difficulty. Having your child listen, hear, and recite nursery rhymes can build confidence, develop prereading skills, and build phonemic awareness."*
>
> —Jillian Zimmerman, first-grade teacher

Do These Words Rhyme?

Do These Words Rhyme? is another listening game that can be done whenever you and your child are together, such as when traveling in the car. It can also be a fun mealtime or bedtime activity. In this game, you say, "Do these words rhyme: *dress* and *mess*?" If your child confirms the rhyme, you can say, "Right! *Dress* and *mess* rhyme because they sound the same at the end." Then try another example, such as "Do these words rhyme: *cave* and *brave*?" Continue to practice word pairs that do rhyme for several weeks before using word pairs that don't rhyme, as they will be harder for your child to perceive. If your child makes an error, you can correct her gently by saying, "Do these words rhyme: *plant* and *plan*?" If your child says yes, simply say, "That's a good guess, but they don't rhyme because they don't sound the same at the end. *Plant* ends with the *t* sound, and *plan* ends with the *n* sound." Then continue to practice words that do rhyme for another few weeks. A variation of this listening game is having your child ask you if word pairs rhyme.

Making Rhymes

After your child can quickly and easily hear whether or not words rhyme by practicing with many different examples, it is time to move on to asking her to generate a rhyming word in response to your example. In this case, you could say something like "What rhymes with *game?*" Hopefully, your child will be able to generate one or more of many correct answers, such as *came, lame, name, same, tame, blame,* and *maim.* A fun variation of this game is to take turns generating as many rhyming words as possible for any sample word.

> "Here is an activity that I recommend for strengthening auditory processing: 'Let's Make a Rhyme.' Say, 'Let's make a rhyme for the word _____.' (Example: rug/bug or bake/rake) When your child suggests a word that does not rhyme, respond with an encouraging phrase, then say both words, emphasizing the beginning sound that changes to make the words rhyme. For early success, focus on one or two word families (e.g., -at, -ig, -op) at a time."
>
> —Eileen Kinney, kindergarten teacher

Strengthening Your Child's Ability to Perceive and Generate Beginning, Ending, and Medial Sounds

Once your child masters the rhyming activities, you can begin to focus on her ability to hear individual sounds (phonemes) within words. Since individual sounds are the smallest, and therefore the hardest to hear, units of sound in the English language, we always wait to work on them until children master the auditory processing of larger units, or words within sentences, described previously. The optimal sequence for helping children process individual sounds within words is to first teach beginning sounds, followed by final sounds, and ending with medial sounds. This instructional sequence reflects the increasing difficulty of these subskills.

Beginning Sounds: Same or Different?

A great listening activity with which to start the processing of individual beginning sounds is to say two words and ask your child if they start with the same or different sounds. For example, you can say, "I'm going to say two words, and I want you to tell me if they start with the same sound: *bug . . . banana.*" If your child completes this task correctly, you can praise him. If your child makes an error, try to gently correct him by emphasizing the first sound in both words. Continue to practice this activity until your child can quickly, easily, and consistently identify whether or not the first sounds of two words are the same or different. Be sure to practice with words that start with the full range of all the sounds of our language.

Beginning Sounds: Generate the Same

After your child can quickly, easily, and consistently complete this activity, begin to help your child generate her own words that start with the same sound as a word that you say. For example, you can ask, "Can you say a word that starts with the same sound as *donkey*?" If your child correctly generates a word that starts with the same sound, congratulate her and say something like, "Great job! *Donkey* and *dog* both start with the sound *d* [make the sound of letter *d*]!" If your child makes a mistake, you can say something like, "Good try, but *donkey* starts with the sound *d*, and *horse* starts with the sound *h*.'" Continue to practice this task until your child can quickly, easily, and consistently generate words that start with the same initial sound that your word has. Again, be sure to practice with words that start with the full range of all the sounds of our language.

Ending Sounds: Same or Different?

Once your child has mastered hearing and generating the beginning sounds in words, you can progress to activities that focus on the final sounds in words. For the activity Ending Sounds: Same or Different? say two words and ask your child if they end with the same sound. For example, you can say, "Listen closely to the words *bear* and *car*. Do they end in the same sound?" Praise your child if she can correctly answer you. If she makes a mistake, repeat the words, emphasizing the last sound in each one and clarifying whether they are the same or different. Continue practicing this task until your child can easily, quickly, and consistently determine whether or not the ending sounds in two words are the same or different.

Ending Sounds: Generate the Same

After your child masters hearing and generating ending sounds for words you suggest, begin to help your child generate his own words that *end* with the same sound as a word that you say. For example, you can say, "Can you say a word that ends the same as *train*?" If your child correctly generates a word that ends with the same sound, congratulate him and say something like, "Great job! *Train* and *man* both end with n [make the sound of the letter n]!" If you child makes a mistake, you can say something like, "Good try, but *train* ends with n and *truck* ends with k." Continue to practice this task until your child can quickly, easily, and consistently generate words that end with the same final sound as your word.

Medial Sounds: Same or Different?

Medial sounds (sounds in the middle of words) are typically the hardest for children to hear, and for this reason we wait to address this auditory processing subskill until the child is proficient with easier listening activities. To being this activity, say something like, "Today we are going to listen to the middle sounds in words and try to figure out if they are the same or different. Are the words *pig* and *hill* the same in the middle?" If your child correctly answers that these words have the same middle sound, praise her and continue to generate word pairs that are the same or different in their middle sounds. If your child gives an incorrect answer for this activity, say something like "Good try, but they are the same in the middle. *Pig* and *hill* both have the sound *i* in the middle (make the sound of a short *i*)." Restate the words emphasizing the same middle sounds of short *i* so that your child can hear them. Then continue to generate word pairs that have the same or different middle sounds until she can easily, quickly, consistently, and correctly discriminate between the same and different medial sounds.

"Here is an activity that I recommend for strengthening auditory processing: 'Name the Sound.' Say, 'Name the beginning sound that you hear in the word _____.' One-syllable words are a perfect place to start, such as map, fog, *or* sit. *Emphasize the focus sound. Once your child has gained confidence, practice naming the ending sound and then the middle or vowel sound of a word. Provide examples and model the procedure of the game by asking your child to say a word and responding by naming the sound that you hear. Taking turns enhances the learning experience and increases the duration of the activity."*

—Eileen Kinney, kindergarten teacher

Medial Sounds: Generate the Same

After your child masters hearing and generating medial sounds for the words you suggest, begin to help him generate his own words that have the same middle sound as a word that you say. For example, you can ask, "Can you say a word that has the same middle sound as *cake*?" If your child correctly generates a word that has the same middle sound, congratulate her and say something like, "Great job! *Cake* and *rain* both have the same middle sound *a* [make the long *a* sound]." Remember that this pairing is correct because, even though the words are from different word families, they sound the same in the middle. If your child makes a mistake you can say something like, "Good try, but *cake* has the long *a* sound in the middle, and *cat* has a short *a* sound in the middle." Continue to practice this task until your child can quickly, easily, and consistently generate words that have the same medial sound as the word that you offer.

Strengthening Your Child's Ability to Manipulate Sounds within Words

The final category of activities for strengthening auditory processing is manipulating sounds within words. In the following activities, your child will strengthen her skill in both listening to and changing auditory information.

Syllable Deletion

This activity is based on the use of compound words that are composed of two complete words, such as *playground* and *cupcake*. The activity will work best if you have a list of compound words ready to use before you begin. These lists can be easily found on the Internet. Once you have your list ready, tell your child that you are going to play a listening game in which part of a word is removed, and he needs to figure out what part of the word remains. It's helpful to give an example, such as "If I say the word *playground*, and take away *play, ground* is left." Then begin by saying, "If I say the word *cupcake* and take away *cup*, what's left?" Continue with this activity until your child can quickly, easily, and consistently remove the first part of a compound word. Then practice removing the second part of a compound word, such as in the example "If I say the word *blackboard* and take away *board*, what's left?"

Beginning Sound Deletion

Beginning sound deletion is the next task in this sequence. Tell your child that you're going to play a listening game in which the first sound of a word is removed, and she needs to figure out what part of the word remains. Then provide an example, such as "If I say the word *pig* and take away the *p* [make the sound of the letter *p*], *ig* is left." Then begin by saying, "If I say the word *hot* and take away the *h* [make the sound of the letter *h*], what's left?" Continue with this activity until your child can quickly, easily, and consistently remove the first sound of words.

Ending Sound Deletion

Ending sound deletion is played the same way as beginning sound deletion, except that the last sound of the word is removed. Tell your child that you're going to play a listening game, in which the last sound of a word is removed, and he needs to figure out what part of the word remains. Then provide an example, such as "If I say the word *house* and take away the *s* [make the sound of the letter *s*], *hou* is left." Then begin by saying, "If I say the word *shirt* and take away the *t* [make the sound of the letter *t*], what's left?" Continue with this activity until your child can quickly, easily, and consistently remove the last sound of words.

Beginning Sound in a Consonant Blend Deletion

A similar activity involves removing the first sound in a consonant blend. Consonant blends are two letters that frequently occur together in the English language, with each retaining its own sound, such as *bl, br, cl, cr, dr, fl,* and *gl*. Again, tell your child that you're going to play a listening game, in which the first sound of a word is removed and she needs to figure out what part of the word remains. Then provide an example, such as "If I say the word *clay* and take away the *c* [make the sound of the letter *c*], *lay* is left." Then begin by saying, "If I say the word *slid* and take away the *s* [make the sound of the letter *s*], what's left?" Continue with this activity until your child can quickly, easily, and consistently remove the first sound of words that start with a consonant blend.

Beginning Sound Substitution

In the beginning sound substitution activity, you and your child can practice changing the first sound in words. Here's a suggested example: "If I say the word *cow* and change the *c* [make the *c* sound] to an *h* [make the *h* sound], what's left?" Continue with this activity until your child can quickly, easily, and consistently change the first sound of words.

Ending Sound Substitution

In the ending sound substitution activity, you and your child can practice changing the last sound in words. Here's a suggested example: "Today we're going to practice changing the last sound in words. For example, if I say the word *big* and change the *g* [make the *g* sound] to an *n* [make the *n* sound], the word *bin* is left. Then begin, "If I say the word *pill* and

> "Here is an activity that I recommend for strengthening auditory processing: March the Syllables. Say, 'We are going to march the syllables in the word _____.' Mention how each marching step flows with the rhythm of the word, then demonstrate the procedure. March is a one-syllable word so you will say the word, then take one marching step; ro/bot has two syllables and two marching steps; di/no/saur has three syllables with three marching steps."
>
> —Eileen Kinney, kindergarten teacher

change the *ll* [make the *l* sound] to an *n* [make the *n* sound], what's left?" Continue with this activity until your child can quickly, easily, and consistently change the last sound of words.

Middle Sound Substitution

In the middle sound substitution activity, you and your child can practice changing the sound in words. Here's a suggested example: "Today we're going to practice changing the middle sound in words. For example, if I say the word *pet* and change the *e* [make the *e* sound] to an *a* [make the *a* sound], the word *pat* is left." Then begin, "If I say the word *tug* and change the *u* [make the short *u* sound] to an *a* [make the short *a* sound], what's left?" Continue with this activity until your child can quickly, easily, and consistently change the middle sound of words.

Chapter Highlights

Auditory processing weakness is the most common cause of reading difficulty. The term *auditory processing* refers to the way in which sounds are processed in the brain, regardless of how well a child hears. Your child may have perfectly normal hearing but still have difficulty with auditory processing. The ability to hear a song but not be able to decipher the lyrics is offered as an example of what an auditory processing weakness feels like to a child. Auditory processing is central to reading because reading is largely based on a process of matching print and sounds. If a child is having difficulty perceiving specific sounds, she will have difficulty matching sounds with print. Therefore, it's important to know how to help your child in this area. First, consult a hearing specialist to rule out any hearing problems. Then engage your child in the activities presented in the chapter to strengthen her auditory processing subskills. The activities include listening for words within sentences; perceiving and generating rhyming words; perceiving and generating beginning, ending, and medial sounds within words; and manipulating sounds within words. Auditory processing activities should be done as *listening-only* activities that are sequenced for difficulty. They do not involve using printed materials. Moreover, it is essential to remember that your child's eating, sleeping, exercising, emotional, and behavioral patterns all greatly influence how well her brain can process auditory information. Tips for how to help your child develop healthy patterns in these foundational areas underlying auditory processing are presented in Chapter 2.

7

What Should I Do If My Child Is Having Difficulty with Phonics?

If I wasn't dyslexic, I probably wouldn't have won the Games. If I had been a better reader, then that would have come easily . . . and I never would have realized that the way you get ahead in life is hard work.

—CAITLYN JENNER (overcame reading
difficulty to become an Olympic gold
medalist and actor)

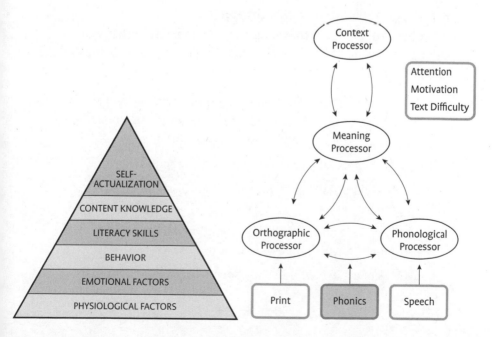

This chapter can help you and your child if:

❑ A professional has told you that your child has phonics difficulty.

❑ You've used the Phonics Skills Checklist in Chapter 4 to determine that your child has phonics difficulty.

❑ Or you're seeing signs that might point to a phonics difficulty, such as:

- Your child has difficulty "sounding out" words when reading.
- Your child has difficulty spelling when writing.

In this chapter I will:

1. Help you understand the term *phonics* and its importance to reading.

2. Provide you with activities and resources that can help you help your child strengthen her phonics skills.

Before you get started on this chapter . . .

Check off all of the following items to make sure that your child's brain is optimally prepared for phonics. *If you can't say "yes" to any item, refer back to Chapter 2.*

❑ My child usually eats a diet high in vegetables and fruits and low in processed foods (food packaged in a box or bag that contains more than one ingredient).

❑ My child usually gets 8–10 hours of sleep per night.

❑ My child usually gets at least 1 hour of vigorous physical activity per day.

❑ My child is able to feel, talk about, and appropriately manage a wide range of emotions.

❑ My child's behavior usually seems focused and on task.

✦ ✦ ✦

What Is Phonics?

Phonics refers to a reader's ability to match print and sound. As discussed in Chapter 5, accurate print identification is produced by a reader's visual processing system, and as we learned in Chapter 6, accurate sound identification is produced by a reader's auditory processing system. Phonics is the ability to accurately match the output of these two systems.

How Important Is Phonics to the Reading Process?

Phonics skill, or the ability to quickly, easily, and consistently match letters with their corresponding sounds, is an essential component of the reading process. Strong phonics skills are associated with higher reading comprehension, higher motivation to read, and higher reading achievement overall. In contrast, weak phonics skills are associated with lower reading comprehension, lower motivation to read, and lower reading achievement in general (*Creating Literacy Instruction for All Students,* Gunning, 2016).

How Common Is Phonics Difficulty?

Phonics difficulty is very common among children with reading challenges because a reader's phonics skill depends on his auditory processing skill. In other words, a reader who is having difficulty hearing sounds within words will not be able to easily, quickly, and consistently match sounds with print. Since many children who have a reading difficulty have trouble with their auditory/sound processing system, their ability to match print and sound with little effort is, consequently, usually negatively affected.

How Can I Help My Child Overcome Phonics Difficulty?

The first step in helping your child overcome phonics challenges is to determine the cause or causes of the difficulty. As discussed in depth in

> *"My son and I practice phonics with a game called Mystery Bag. I put assorted objects in a bag, and he picks them out one at a time. Then he has to say the word for the object and find the matching magnetic letter on the refrigerator that starts the word. As he got better at phonics, we moved to focusing on the last sound/letter of the word. It worked really well."*
>
> —Benson Roy, father of a struggling reader

Chapter 4, the potential causes of a phonics problem are: (1) difficulty processing print (which impedes accurate print and sound matching); (2) difficulty processing sound (which impedes accurate print and sound matching); and (3) difficulty with accurate print and sound matching. Your child may have difficulty in any one or all of these areas. Before you start to work with your child on the activities presented in this chapter, I highly recommend reviewing the section on monitoring your child's phonics ability in Chapter 4 to determine the specific source of your child's phonics difficulty. In my opinion, difficulty in processing print should be addressed by using the recommendations and activities in Chapter 5 before proceeding with this chapter. Likewise, difficulty in processing sounds should be addressed by using the recommendations and activities in Chapter 6 before proceeding here. Once you have determined that your child is proficient in processing both print and sounds by using the ideas presented in Chapters 4 through 6, phonics activities can begin.

To start, it is helpful to know a few phonics terms that educators and reading researchers use: *consonants, long vowels, short vowels, consonant blends, digraphs,* and *diphthongs.*

> *"I am a big believer in multisensory approaches to instruction. In my opinion, a strictly visually based technique to teaching words is not enough. I integrate phonemic awareness, letter–sound skills, and word study into of all of my instruction. When I do this, I observe my students improving their overall reading."*
>
> —Jessica Warner, K–2 reading specialist, literacy coach, and Wilson 1 certified personal tutor

> *"It is often helpful to use visualizing techniques when children have challenges reading. In this, children are asked to see in their minds the letter that makes a particular sound and the words formed by particular letters. For this to be effective, children must first thoroughly understand the sounds that are represented by letters. While instruction once placed letter identification and letter naming first, experts now find that a strong foundation in sounds is critical for reading and will support all struggling readers, particularly those who struggle with visual processing."*
>
> —Dr. Christine Lopez, educator and consultant

✦ *Consonants* are speech sounds that are made with your mouth mostly closed. There are 21 consonants in the English language made by the letters *b, c, d, f, g, h, j, k, l, m, n, p, q, r, s, t, v, x, z,* and usually *w* and *y.*

✦ *Long Vowels* are speech sounds that are made with your mouth mostly open. Long vowels say the name of the letter (for example, the *a* in the word *game* is long because it says its name). The vowels are *a, e, i, o, u,* and sometimes *y.*

✦ *Short* Vowels are speech sounds that are made with your mouth mostly open that do not say their own name (for example, the *a* in *sat* is short because it does not say its name). Whether they are short or long, the vowels are *a, e, i, o, u,* and sometimes *y.*

✦ *Consonant Blends* are two consonants that often appear together in the English language, in which both consonants can be heard. The most common beginning consonant blends are *bl, cl, fl, gl, pl, sl, br, cr, dr, fr, gr, pr, tr, wr, sc, sk, sm, sn, sp, st, sw, sch, scr, squ, str, spr, spl, shr, dw, tw,* and *thr* (*The New Reading Teacher's Book of Lists*, Fry & Kress, 2006).

> *"My son loves to be on the iPad, so, as much as possible, I try to use it to help him with phonics. For example, if he is searching for a specific YouTube video, I make him figure out the letters of the words of the video. It's amazing how much he can read when he's trying to find something that he wants!"*
>
> —Cynthia Shui, mother of a struggling reader

"I am an advocate of using a multisensory teaching approach to encourage the understanding of sounds and text. Some examples include body movement (both gross and fine motor), manipulating objects, and repetitive games."

—Tara M. Jakubowski, MA, Usborne Books and More,
Senior Executive Leader, Wilson Reading certified instructor

✦ *Digraphs* are also two consonants that often appear together in the English language. However, in contrast to consonant blends, in which both consonants are heard, in digraphs the two consonants work together to produce a new sound. The common English digraphs are *ch, sh, wh,* and *th.*

✦ *Diphthongs* are two vowels that often appear together in the English language. The common English diphthongs are *ai, ay, ea, ee, oa, oi, oo, ou,* and *oy.*

Another important point to remember when getting ready to strengthen your child's phonics skills is to progress from the easiest to the most difficult letter–sound matches. Phonics skill is like any other skill; it is best taught from easiest to most difficult. I've organized the activities for strengthening your child's phonic skills in this manner—from easiest to hardest. Be sure that your child can easily and quickly complete all of the beginning phonics activities before progressing to the more difficult ones.

Activities to Strengthen Phonics Skills

Beginning Consonant Activities

The most common starting point for teaching consonant print and sound matching is to have children look at pictures, or picture cards, with accompanying words that emphasize the *beginning consonant* in the word. For example, for the beginning consonant *b* the child is shown a picture and the accompanying word for objects such as *ball, bat, bull, broom,* and *bee.* Each printed word that accompanies the picture should highlight the target beginning consonant, in this instance, **B***all,* **B***at,* **B***ull,* **B***room,* and **B***ee.* The words accompanying the pictures can also be presented in the lowercase, such as *ball, bat, bull, broom,* and *bee.* The sequence in which beginning consonant sounds can be taught can follow the alphabet: *b, c, d, f, g, h, j, k, l, m, n, p, q, r, s, t, v, x, z,* and usually *w* and *y.* You can make the materials at home to teach beginning print and sound consonant matching, but it's usually more time and cost effective to purchase them. There are several hands-on books and materials that can be purchased to help you teach your child beginning consonant letter and sound matching.

✦ *Explode the Code Felt Wall Chart and Explode the Code Wall Chart Activity Book.* Both published by School Specialty (schoolspecialty .com), the *Explode the Code Felt Wall Chart* and accompanying activity book (purchased separately) provide 40 hands-on games and activities for teaching the connection between initial consonant letters and their corresponding sounds. The felt chart is constructed of 26 small pockets, each featuring a letter of the alphabet. There is also a small object or animal to fit in each pocket (for example, an *apple* for letter A, a *banana* for letter B, a *cat* for letter C, and a *duck* for letter D). If purchased alone, the felt chart can be hung on the wall, and you and your child can enjoy matching each of the objects with the pocket that corresponds to its starting letter sound. The supplementary activity book provides additional ideas for using the wall chart and objects.

✦ *Wilson Language Basics Keyword Poster and Keyword Puzzles.* Published by Wilson Language Basics (wilsonlanguage.com), a leader in phonics-based instructional materials, the *Pre-K Basic Keyword Poster* highlights a key picture and accompanying word for each letter of the alphabet (such as a picture of a *mitten* for the letter M). This poster is an ideal decoration for any child's bedroom or play space. Sold separately, *Keyword Puzzles* feature the same key pictures and are constructed so that your child can assemble the picture with its matching beginning letter sound.

Beginning Consonant Books

Next, I discuss the same five books that I recommended in Chapter 5 for reinforcing letter names. These books can now be used to highlight the connection between the printed letter and sound of each of the highlighted words in the alphabet books.

✦ *Eating the Alphabet: Fruits and Vegetables from A to Z* (Lois Ehlert, 1989). This text provides colorful illustrations and accompanying names of fruits and vegetables for all the letters of the alphabet (for example, *B* for *Broccoli* and *C* for *Cantaloupe*). When using this book to strengthen phonics skills, be sure to draw your child's attention to the connections between the picture, the word, the beginning letter, and the beginning sound of each fruit and vegetable. Here's an example of what you can say: "This is a picture of broccoli, and this word says broccoli. Broccoli starts with the letter *B* that says the sound *B* [emphasize the *B* sound]." In this example, you can see how the academic words (words commonly used in schools) *picture, word, letter,* and *sound* are all emphasized. Helping your child master academic words will be an additional boost to his academic achievement (*Creating Literacy Instruction for All Students,* Gunning, 2016).

✦ *D is for Dump Truck: A Construction Alphabet* (Michael Shoulders, 2016). *B* is for Bulldozer, *D* is for Dump Truck, *F* is for Front-End Loader! If your child loves the world of construction, this is the book for your family. Strengthen your child's phonics skills while helping her read the names of favorite construction vehicles and tools. Remember to emphasize the academic terms—*picture, word, letter,* and *sound*—as you reinforce the matching of beginning consonants and their corresponding sounds for each picture.

✦ *ABC Dream* (Kim Krans, 2013). Try this book featuring intriguing pen and ink drawings highlighted with watercolors for a quieter time activity. Each page contains a different letter and pictures of animals and objects that start with that letter. Continue to emphasize the connections of beginning letters and beginning sounds as you and your child share this lovely text.

In addition to sharing hands-on activities and books, here are three free downloadable online activities for reinforcing beginning letter and sound correspondences from *The Measured Mom* (themeasuredmom .com) website.

✦ **Beginning Sounds Picture Mats and Cards.** This activity consists of 25 picture mats and matching letter cards. The first picture mat focuses on the beginning letters and accompanying sounds *T* and *F*. The pictures on the picture mat are of a *fan, tent, fire, toothbrush, turtle, feet, flag,* and *tape*. Using the letter cards, your child decides which letter starts the word for each picture. Each picture mat following the first one becomes progressively more difficult.

✦ **Beginning Sounds Alphabet Game.** This game consists of an alphabet game board and alphabet picture cards. Each player draws a picture card, determines the beginning sound and letter of the word that represents that picture, and moves his game piece to the corresponding letter on the board. Reminiscent of the famous childhood game Candy Land, the first player to reach the end of the alphabet path wins.

✦ **Beginning Sounds Parking Lot.** If you have a child who loves matchbox cars and has a hefty collection of them, this game is for you. Using your child's car collection, attach a white sticker (or a small piece of white first aid tape) to the top of each car, and print one consonant letter on the white sticker or tape. Then use the free downloadable worksheets showing pictures of objects to help your child "drive" each matchbox car to the correct parking space. Make sure to emphasize the beginning letters and corresponding sounds as you complete this fun activity.

Ending Consonants Activities

After your child has mastered beginning consonant phonics, progress to ending sound phonics. The purpose of these activities is to help your child develop proficiency in matching the letter at the end of words with the sound to which it corresponds. Here are some activities and books to help you achieve this goal.

✦ *Ending Sounds Matching Puzzles,* created by Fun Express and available online, contains self-correcting puzzle pieces that children use to match pictures of objects that end with the same sound.

✦ *Pop and Match Ending Sounds Game Box,* created by Lakeshore and available online, includes write and wipe game cards showing pictures of objects and the beginning letters of the corresponding word (for example, a picture of a *fan* with the letters *f* and *a* already printed). Players take turns using a little device to "pop" dice that show ending consonants. The first player to correctly complete all of his words with the missing ending consonant wins.

✦ *Ending Sound Bingo* can be downloaded and printed for free from the website teacherspayteachers.com. The game consists of boards containing a variety of pictures plus consonant letter cards. Players take turns choosing letter cards and marking the pictures of objects that end with that letter sound.

Ending Consonants Books

Although there doesn't seem to be a wide variety of books specifically oriented to emphasizing ending phonics sounds, books that emphasize rhyming are good reinforcers for the skill. Three classic rhyming books are *Miss Mary Mack: A Hand-Clapping Rhyme* (Hoberman & Westcott, 2003); *There Was an Old Lady Who Swallowed a Fly* (Taback, 1997); and *Tikki Tikki Tembo* (Mosel, 2007). For parents who want a workbook that emphasizes ending consonants, *Final Consonant Sounds: Phonics in Action* (Beals & Beals, 2001) is a good choice.

Short-Vowel Activities

After your child has mastered beginning and ending consonant phonics, it is time to progress to short-vowel phonics activities. Short-vowel phonics activities are often difficult for children because the short-vowel sounds of *a, e, i, o,* and *u* are all fairly similar. Children need to listen really carefully, and get a lot of practice, to learn which short-vowel sound matches the corresponding letter. These three activities (all available from Lakeshore) can be a big help in getting your child to master this skill.

✦ *Word Building Puzzles* contains the puzzle pieces to create 16 short-vowel words and corresponding pictures. Your child will surely enjoy assembling these picture-word puzzles while reinforcing her short-vowel phonics skills.

✦ *Build-A-Word! Magnet Board—3-Letter Words* provides everything needed for your child to build 36 words using letter magnets, familiar picture magnets, and an 8″-by-10″ activity board designed to help children link picture cards to their corresponding three-letter words.

✦ *Touch and Read CVC Words Match* provides cards with three-letter words clearly spelled out on them. Your child can touch each letter of the word as he reads them, and then locate the picture card that matches each word.

Short-Vowel Books

Reading the following books with your child can reinforce short-vowel sounds. Remember, books do not have to be purchased; they can be borrowed from the library.

+ *Short a*—*The Cat in the Hat* (Seuss, 1957), *Tad and Dad* (Stein, 2015), *Bat and Rat* (Jennings, 2012), and *Splat the Cat* (Scotton, 2012)

+ *Short e*—*Red Sled* (Judge, 2011) and *The Little Red Pen* (Stevens & Crummel, 2019)

+ *Short i*—*Elephant and Piggie: The Complete Collection* (Williams, 2018)

+ *Short o*—*Hop on Pop* (Seuss, 1963) and *Fox in Sox* (Seuss & Geisel, 1965)

+ *Short u*—*The Bug in the Jug Wants a Hug: A Short Vowels Sound Book* (Cleary & Miskimins, 2009).

In addition to these vowel-specific books, *Peppa Phonics Boxed Set* (Scholastic, 2017) includes 10 short *Peppa Pig* stories created specifically to teach short-vowel sounds. The boxed set also includes two phonics workbooks.

Short-Vowel Online Resources

Three free online resources for reinforcing short-vowel sounds can be found and downloaded at *The Measured Mom* (themeasuredmom.com).

+ *Free CVC Clip Cards for Short Vowel Words.* Each card shows a picture of a short-vowel word and a choice of the five short vowels: *a, e, i, o,* and *u.* Using a clothespin, children pin the correct vowel heard in each word.

+ *Roll a Short Vowel Game.* This activity includes a game board depicting a path of pictures of short-vowel words. Players roll dice and move their pieces in correspondence to short-vowel sounds.

+ *35 Hands-on Short Vowel Mats.* This activity includes 35 reading mats, each featuring a different short-vowel word family. Children select the correct picture and word cards that belong in each family.

Long-Vowel Activities

After short vowels are mastered, start to work on long vowels. The following activities can help your child master the matching of vowels with their long-vowel sounds.

+ **Vowel Sounds Magnetic Sorting Tiles** and **Magnetic Write and Wipe Board.** Created by Lakeshore, *Vowel Sounds Magnetic Sorting Tiles* contains 100 magnetic tiles showing pictures and words for long- and short-vowel words. Using the header tiles that specify categories such as short *a* and long *a*, children sort the magnetic tiles into the vowel categories in which they belong. The *Magnetic Write and Wipe Board* is sold separately.

+ *Learning Puzzles: Vowel Sounds,* created by Scholastic, includes 20 five-piece puzzles. Children assemble the puzzles by matching pictures and words that share a common vowel.

+ *Montessori Silent E Reading Blocks,* by Quality Montessori, provide children with hands-on wooden blocks that turn on a spindle to help teach the differences between short- and long-vowel words created by adding the silent *e* (for example, *cub* becomes *cube* and *kit* becomes *kite*).

Long-Vowel Books

In addition to these hands-on activities, you may want to consider sharing the following books with your child.

+ **Pete the Cat Phonics Box** (Dean, 2017). This set contains 12 *Pete the Cat* books written specifically to reinforce short- and long-vowel sounds.
+ **Bob Books Set 5—Long Vowels** (Maslen, 2006). This book emphasizes long vowels and the magic silent *e*.
+ **The Nice Mice in the Rice: A Long Vowel Sounds Book** (Cleary, 2009). As the title indicates, this storybook is also designed specifically to reinforce long-vowel sounds.

Long-Vowel Online Resources

Here are three online games for strengthening children's long-vowel phonics skills.

+ **Readwritethink.org.** *Picture Match Game for Long Vowel Sounds*
+ **Starfall.com.** *Learn to Read Games and Narrated Books: Long A, Long O, and the Amazing Silent E*
+ **Literactive.com.** *The Magic E Machine Game*

Consonant Blend Activities

Moving forward, after your child has mastered the sounds of beginning consonants, ending consonants, short vowels, and long vowels using the silent (magic) *e*, it's time to begin consonant blends. As a reminder, consonant blends are two letters that frequently occur together in the English language, in which you can hear both sounds of the letters.

Examples of consonant blends are *bl, dr,* and *sm.* Here are some hands-on materials that you can purchase to help your child master consonant blend phonics.

✦ **Beginning Consonant Blends Puzzles and Game,** designed by Creative Educational, contains 25 self-correcting puzzles, each featuring a different consonant blend. A consonant blend game is also included in the package.

✦ **Meet the Phonics Blends Flashcards** (Oxley, 2012) is a set of cards that focuses on phonics blends. One side of each card has a picture of an object and its corresponding word. The other side of the card shows the picture, and the child fills in the missing blend. There is also an accompanying workbook, *Meet the Phonics Blend Workbook* (Oxley, 2013), which is sold separately.

Consonant Blend Books

Books to read with your child that emphasize consonant blends include:

✦ *Slowly, Slowly, Slowly, said the Sloth* (Carle, 2007)

✦ *Stop, Drop, and Flop in the Slop: A Short Vowel Sounds Book with Consonant Blends* (Cleary, 2009)

✦ *Some Smug Slug* (Edwards, 1998)

Consonant Blend Online Resources

The following three great websites provide online consonant blend activities and books:

✦ **Reading A to Z** (ReadingA-Z.com) is an extremely popular educational website that has some materials available for free and others available with a subscription. Insert the term "blends" in the search bar to locate targeted activities and blend-focused, easy-to-read books.

✦ **ABC Mouse** (ABCMouse.com) also has some activities available for free and others available with a subscription. After opening an account, select from the Phonics Activities or from the more than 450 available books for beginning readers.

✦ **ABCYa!** (ABCYa.com) has a free game for practicing consonant blends called *Fuzz Bug Farm*.

Digraph Activities

Digraphs follow blends in the phonics-teaching sequence. In contrast to blends, in which two frequently paired consonants can both be heard, digraphs are two frequently paired consonants that create a new sound (*ch*, *sh*, and *th*). Digraphs can be tricky for children to master. These hands-on materials can help.

✦ *Pete the Cat Purrfect Pairs Game: Beginning Blends and Digraphs,* by Edupress, features word cards with 24 different beginning blends and digraphs. Players match word cards that begin similarly to win.

✦ *Didax Reading Skills Puzzles: Consonant Blends and Digraphs* contains 30 puzzles in which children match beginning consonant blends and digraphs pictures and words.

✦ *Educational Insights Hot Dots Phonics Flash Cards: Blends and Digraphs,* by Learning Resources, offers 36 double-sided cards with pictures and corresponding fill-in-the-blank blends and digraphs.

Digraph Books

Books emphasizing consonant digraphs that can be read with your child include:

✦ *No Sleep for the Sheep!* (Beaumont, 2011)

✦ *Thump, Thump, Rat-a-Tat-Tat* (Baer, 1989)

✦ *Blue Chicken* (Freedman, 2011)

Digraph Online Resources

The following online activities can also help you help your child learn to master digraphs.

+ **Starfall.com.** Click "Learn to Read" to find free online games for teaching the *sh, wh, th,* and *ch* digraphs.

+ **Literactive.com.** Sign in and click "Road to Reading" to find an assortment of online phonics activities, including those that focus on digraphs.

+ **Themeasuredmom.com.** Use the search bar to find *5 Free Games for Teaching Digraphs.*

Diphthong Activities

Finally(!), the last category of phonics skills that your child needs to master is diphthongs. As defined earlier, diphthongs are two vowels that often appear together in the English language, such as *ai* and *oa*. Some hands-on diphthong teaching materials that you can purchase from Lakeshore include:

+ *Sound-It-Out Vowel Combination Puzzles,* which contains 12 self-correcting puzzles, each featuring a different vowel diphthong.

+ *Vowel Teams Instant Learning Centers: Write and Wipe Cards,* which contains write and wipe word cards on which children add the missing vowel diphthong.

+ *Vowel and Vowel Team Flash Cards,* which contains 24 cards, each highlighting a key vowel or diphthong, and sample words. Six activity cards are also included.

Diphthong Books

To strengthen diphthong knowledge through sharing books with your child, try these two:

+ *The Frail Snail on the Trail: A Long Vowel Sounds Book with Consonant Blends* (Cleary, 2009)

+ *Smooch Your Pooch* (Slater, 2010) and *Things that Float and Things that Don't* (Adler, 2014)

Diphthong Online Resources

The following online activity can also help you help your child learn to master diphthongs:

+ *11 Amazingly Helpful Videos to Teach Vowel Diphthongs to Students.* (ateachableteacher.com/videos-to-teach-diphthongs)

Chapter Highlights

Phonics refers to a reader's ability to match print and sound. Strong phonics skills are a central part of the reading process and are associated with strong reading comprehension, high motivation to read, and high reading achievement overall. Unfortunately, because readers' phonics skills depend on their auditory processing skill, and many children with reading difficulties have trouble with their auditory/sound processing system, phonics difficulty is very common among children with reading challenges. This chapter reviewed the primary phonics relationships that all readers need to learn (consonants, short vowels, long vowels, consonant blends, digraphs, and diphthongs). It also offered guidance in selecting materials, books, and online resources that you can use to help your children master these centrally important reading skills.

8

What Should I Do If My Child Is Having Difficulty with Vocabulary?

I am the American Dream. I am the epitome of what the American Dream basically said. It said you could come from anywhere and be anything you want in this country. That's exactly what I've done. . . . I am where I am because I believe in all possibilities.

—WHOOPI GOLDBERG (overcame reading difficulty to become an actor)

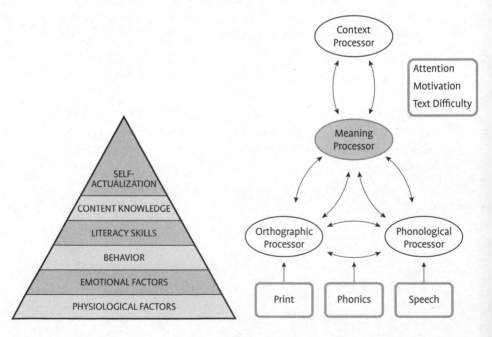

This chapter can help you and your child if:

❑ A professional has told you that your child has vocabulary difficulty.

❑ You've used the Vocabulary Skills Checklist in Chapter 4 to determine that your child has vocabulary difficulty.

❑ Or you're seeing signs that might point to vocabulary difficulty, such as:

- Your child has difficulty understanding what he is reading.

In this chapter I will:

1. Help you understand the term *vocabulary* and its importance to reading.

2. Provide you with activities and resources that can help you help your child strengthen her vocabulary skills.

Before you get started on this chapter . . .

Check off all of the following items to make sure that your child's brain is optimally prepared for learning vocabulary. *If you can't say "yes" to any item, refer back to Chapter 2.*

❑ My child usually eats a diet high in vegetables and fruits and low in processed foods (food packaged in a box or bag that contains more than one ingredient).

❑ My child usually gets 8–10 hours of sleep per night.

❑ My child usually gets at least 1 hour of vigorous physical activity per day.

❑ My child is able to feel, talk about, and appropriately manage a wide range of emotions.

❑ My child's behavior usually seems focused and on task.

✦ ✦ ✦

What Is Vocabulary, and Why Is It Important?

The term *vocabulary* refers to understanding the meaning of words. Much of what we as humans know is organized in our brains as vocabulary. For example, if we know the word *hieroglyphics*, we know what hieroglyphics are. If we know the word *remonstrate*, we know that action. If we know the word *insouciant*, we know that feeling. For every word that we know, we have a corresponding concept in our brain. The more words we know, the more concepts we know. The more concepts we know, the more intelligent we are often judged to be. That's why so many types of standardized tests, from achievement tests for young children to the SATs often required for college entry, and the mandated GREs for graduate school, the LSATs for law school, and the MCATs for medical school, have a vocabulary component. Vocabulary is viewed as a good measure of what, and how much, information a person knows.

In addition to being a route to expanding one's general knowledge, vocabulary has been shown to be essential to understanding what you are reading. If you don't know the meaning of the individual words you're reading, you'll find it very difficult to construct the overall meaning of the sentences, paragraphs, pages, and chapters of the text. Furthermore research has demonstrated that teaching children the key vocabulary words of any specific text will greatly enhance their ability to understand (comprehend) that text. Teaching the meaning of key words in texts *before reading* is a common approach for helping children expand their vocabulary and improving their reading comprehension. Reviewing words *during* and *after reading* will further reinforce your child's understanding of these words.

Most children, and probably most adults too, can benefit from expanding their vocabulary. Some children have a greater difficulty mastering vocabulary because of language, hearing, and learning differences. I offer the following ideas for helping your child increase her vocabulary grouped into two broad categories: (1) ideas for increasing general vocabulary and (2) ideas for learning specific vocabulary for any text.

Ideas for Increasing General Vocabulary

Oral Language Techniques

Research has demonstrated that children learn most of their vocabulary from interacting with their parents. Moreover, studies of precocious children show that their parents use specific language techniques associated with their children's accelerated language development. These techniques are described in the following list. I recommend that you keep these guidelines in mind as much as possible when interacting with your child.

✦ *Add information to what your child is saying.* For example, if your child says, "Look, there's the Statue of Liberty!" you can respond, "That's right. The Statue of Liberty was a gift from the people of France to the people of the United States in 1886. It is made of bronze and created by the sculptor Frederic Auguste Bartholdi." You can see how in this example the child can begin to learn the words *bronze* and *sculptor.* Using sophisticated words as you add information in response to your child's comments is one of the most effective ways to increase vocabulary.

> *"My son always likes when I read to him so, to improve his vocabulary, I read him books on topics that he likes (cars, boats, trains, and airplanes), and then we make vocabulary cards from the words in the books. We save the word cards and then read and discuss them over time. It's amazing how many words my son has learned doing this."*
>
> —Marcy Klein, mother of a struggling reader

✦ *Relate comments to your own life.* One particularly effective way of adding information is to relate what your child is saying to your own life. Using the previous example, if your child says, "Look, there's the Statue of Liberty!" you can respond, "That's right. My parents, your grandparents, remember seeing the Statue of Liberty when they *emigrated* here from Germany in 1940. Since the Statue of Liberty is a *symbol* of *freedom* from *persecution,* seeing it in person upon arriving in the United States was a *profoundly* moving experience for them." Again, it is easy to see how responding to your child's comment by linking it to your personal life can be used as a vehicle for increasing your child's vocabulary.

✦ *Be sure your child understands the vocabulary words you're using.* In these examples, the adult is responding to the child's comments with the use of sophisticated words that can increase his vocabulary. Even though this is a great way to help your child expand his vocabulary, be sure to pay attention to whether or not your child understands the words you're using. If he doesn't seem to understand, restate your comments in easier words.

✦ *Use open-ended questions.* Open-ended questions are those that require more than a single-word response. Examples of open-ended questions are: *What did you do in school today?* (Not, *How was school?*) *What did you work on in math today? What did you do in physical education today? What happened during lunch today? Why is Carmen angry with Anthony?* Open-ended questions give children the opportunity to produce more language than do closed-ended questions (*Did you have a good day?*) and therefore provide an opportunity for increasing their vocabulary.

✦ *Use the "tell-me-about" prompt.* The tell-me-about prompt is another great way to increase your child's language production and vocabulary development. Imagine the difference between saying to your child "How was your day?" (typical answer: "OK" or "Fine") versus "Tell me about your day," in which case you would likely get some kind of summary or short story (e.g., "First we did *xxx*, then we did *xxx*," and so on).

✦ *Encourage your child to master code switching.* Code switching is the ability to speak (and write) in both a cultural dialect and in grammatical Standard English. Children who can mindfully code switch, preserving their familial and cultural language patterns, while also mastering Standard English grammar, have greater academic achievement than children who can speak and write only in their own cultural dialect. You can help your child master code switching by restating her dialectical comments in Standard English. This is also called *modeling* Standard English. Code switching and modeling help expand your child's Standard English vocabulary.

Thematic Learning

Thematic learning means giving your child a variety of experiences related to a topic that interests her. Through these experiences, your child's vocabulary will increase. One possible way to start is for you and your child to choose one thematic topic per month. I list next a few sample thematic topics, activities that can be associated with the topic, and vocabulary words that can be learned. For thematic learning to be optimally effective, be sure to ask for your child's input in selecting the topics.

✦ *Under the Sea*. Read books together on the topic; search the Internet; visit an aquarium, a beach, and a river. Vocabulary expansion can include *algae, abalone, bivalve, barracuda, currents, coral reef, ebb tide, kelp, otter, oyster, plankton, phytoplankton, salinity, seaweed, sponge, tide pool, tide, tsunami,* and *whelk.*

> "To help increase vocabulary, I focus on a child's interests and then create a match game using index cards. I simply make two cards for each vocabulary word, flip them over, and we take turns trying to find the matches. Once a match is found, we focus on decoding the word, and then use it in a sentence to demonstrate understanding. I think this activity is successful because the child is getting game time with an adult, and the word cards are generated from the child's interests."
> —Laurie Levinson, retired teacher

✦ *The Solar System*. Read books together on the topic, search the Internet, visit a planetarium. Vocabulary expansion can include *asteroid, asteroid belt, atmosphere, comet, core, crater, ellipse, gravity, lunar eclipse, meteorite, meteor, orbit, revolution, rotation, satellite, solar eclipse, star,* and *terrestrial.*

✦ *Cooking*. Read books together on the topic; search the Internet, cook together, take cooking classes together. Vocabulary expansion can include *baste, batter, blanch, caramelize, deglaze, dissolve, drizzle, garnish, glaze, julienne, knead, mince, poach, puree, roast, sauté, scald, simmer, skim, snip, strain, whip,* and *zest.*

✦ *Transportation*. Read books together on the topic, search the Internet, visit a transportation museum, use different modes of transportation. Vocabulary expansion can include *aircraft carrier, barge, cabin cruiser, cable car, amphibious vehicle, blimp, bathyscaphe, biplane, bobsled, chariot, convertible, catamaran, crop duster, chairlift, dirigible, funicular vehicle, frigate, gondola, gridlock, hydrofoil, hatchback, hearse, hovercraft, hybrid, jalopy, kayak, minesweeper, moped, propeller, rickshaw, roadster, schooner, sedan, transit, trolley, toboggan, Vespa, windjammer, yacht, yawl, zeppelin,* and *Zamboni.*

Word Study

You may also want to help your child expand his vocabulary through *systematic word study.* Systematic word study involves investigations of prefixes, suffixes, root words, synonyms, and antonyms as paths to increasing word meaning knowledge. For example, the prefixes *dis-, in-, im-, il-, ir-, re-,* and *un-* account for 97% of all prefixed words. Likewise, the suffixes *-ed, -ing, -ion, -tion, -ation, -ition, -ly, -s,* and *-es* account for 97% of all suffixed words. Therefore, learning the meanings of this small group of affixes has a strong payoff for your child. Similarly, common root words, synonyms, and antonyms can be found online. Two great online resources for word study are Flocabulary.com and Playwordcraft.com. Beloved by teachers, Flocabulary is a subscription-based website that provides hip-hop-based videos and activities for K–12 vocabulary learning across content areas. Wordcraft improves viewers' vocabulary through online games based on the study of Greek and Latin root words.

Creating an At-Home Environment That Celebrates Vocabulary

Creating an at-home environment that celebrates vocabulary learning is one of the most beneficial approaches that you can take to support your child's cognitive and academic growth. Celebrating vocabulary learning at home means emphasizing the meaning of words and encouraging and

> *"We keep a notebook of new, interesting words that my son learns. Sometimes he draws pictures to go with the words. Then, every now and then, we read the book. It's really nice because he made the book, so he's always successful reading and knowing the words."*
> —Valentina Martinez, mother of a struggling reader

praising the learning of new words. Here are three ideas that can help you attain this goal.

✦ *Word of the day.* To create a word-of-the-day practice in your home, simply create 30 or so index cards per month, each featuring a word you would like your child to learn. Each day, show the word to your child in the morning and the evening, discussing it with her. Be sure to periodically review already learned words. You may also want to provide positive reinforcement to your child for using the newly learned words in conversation or writing. To do this, add a penny to a glass jar each time your child correctly uses a newly learned vocabulary word. When the jar is full, give the pennies to your child, or let her select a special outing or treat.

✦ *Shared reading.* Another ideal way to celebrate vocabulary learning is to pay special attention to vocabulary words during shared reading. Be sure to talk about any words that you feel may be unfamiliar to your child.

✦ *Word games.* Playing games, such as *Scrabble,* and completing crossword puzzles with your child will also contribute to an at-home environment that celebrates word learning. If you emphasize word learning and have fun doing so, your child will too.

Ideas for Learning Specific Vocabulary for Texts

As explained at the beginning of this chapter, understanding the meaning of individual words within a text has been shown to be essential to understanding what you're reading. Here are my suggestions for a few activities that can help your child learn unfamiliar words associated with any text.

Before Reading

Before reading a new text, take a few minutes to peruse the reading material to identify 8–10 words that you think might be unfamiliar to your child. Make a list of these words and then review them with your child. Make sure that he looks at each word and knows how to say it. Then discuss the meaning of the word using child-friendly definitions. After you present each definition, discuss the word for a few minutes. For instance, if you're teaching the word *Lepidoptera*, explain to your child that it is a category of insects that includes both butterflies and moths. Then discuss Lepidoptera. What do they look like? Where do they live? What do they eat? How do they procreate? If your child is interested, you can search online for pictures and information about Lepidoptera. Perhaps each time you read a new piece of text, you can choose one of the 8–10 words to investigate more fully online. Extended discussions of unknown words prior to reading will reinforce to your child the importance of vocabulary in general and provide him with a deep understanding of new words.

During Reading

If you use the before-reading ideas, your child may be excited to find his newly acquired word as he reads. Each time you come across a newly learned word, I suggest pausing the reading for a moment to discuss the word again. As you read, you may also come across additional unknown words. Be sure to stop to discuss any unfamiliar words.

After Reading

After reading is the time to review your child's newly learned words. Here are a few activities that will reinforce your child's learning of new vocabulary words from any text.

1. *Flash card practice.* Using homemade flash cards, show your child each word. Have her read the word and explain what it means.

2. *Create a matching worksheet.* On one side of the worksheet, list the newly learned words. On the other side of the worksheet, list the newly learned definitions. See if your child can correctly match the words and definitions.

3. *Sentence creation.* Help your child create and write a sentence for each newly learned word.

4. *Semantic map.* Create a semantic map (see the example in the diagram below) for each newly learned vocabulary word. A semantic map is an organized visual presentation of a target word and its related conceptual knowledge. For example, a semantic map for *Lepidoptera* features the word *Lepidoptera* in the center of the map and the categories related to the conceptual knowledge of Lepidoptera on the perimeter of the map. Categories of conceptual knowledge could include the types, habitats, food choices, and life cycles of Lepidoptera. Once you have created the shell of the semantic map (the word in the middle of map and the categories of related conceptual knowledge on the map's perimeter), help your child add the detailed information.

5. *Semantic feature analysis chart.* Create a sematic feature analysis chart (see the example in the diagram on the next page) for closely related vocabulary words. A semantic feature analysis chart lists the vocabulary words on the left side of the chart and the features related to each of the vocabulary words across the top of the chart. For example, a semantic feature analysis chart on *Lepidoptera* lists the types of butterflies and moths on the left side of the chart and characteristics related to moths and butterflies (color, number of wings, food eaten, and habitat) across the top of the chart. Your child then checks off which features are related to each specific butterfly and moth.

Semantic Map for Lepidoptera

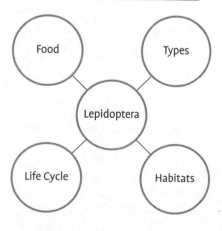

Semantic Feature Analysis for Lepidoptera

Lepidoptera	Butterfly or moth?	Color?	Number of wings?	Food eaten?	Habitat?
Monarch					
Luna					
Gypsy					
Black swallowtail					
Atlas					
Painted lady					

6. *Venn diagram.* Create a Venn diagram (see the example below) to help your child understand the similarities and differences between two closely related words. A Venn diagram is a graphic depiction of two overlapping circles. In the area of overlap, write the overlapping vocabulary words, such as *Lepidoptera, butterflies,* and *moths.* Then, on the left side of the overlapping circles, write the word *butterflies,* and on the right side of

Venn Diagram for Lepidoptera

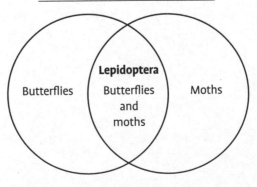

the overlapping circle write the word *moths*. Help your child add detailed information related specifically to butterflies and specifically to moths on each side of the diagram.

7. *Online investigation.* Take time to electronically investigate the 10 new vocabulary words. As your child looks at, reads about, and discusses his new vocabulary words, his understanding and memory for each new word will grow in depth and breadth.

Chapter Highlights

Much of what we know is organized in our brains as vocabulary—our understanding of the meaning of words. The more words—and therefore concepts—that we know, the more intelligent we are often judged to be. Vocabulary not only helps us expand our general knowledge, but also is essential to understanding what we read. This chapter provided a variety of ideas for increasing your child's general vocabulary knowledge, from carefully crafted ways of talking with your child to focusing on thematic learning, using systematic word study, and creating a home environment that celebrates word learning. The chapter also described activities you can do before, during, and after reading to help your child master text-specific vocabulary words.

9

What Should I Do If My Child Is Having Difficulty with Reading Comprehension?

The noblest pleasure is the joy of understanding.

—LEONARDO DA VINCI (overcame reading difficulty to become an artist and inventor)

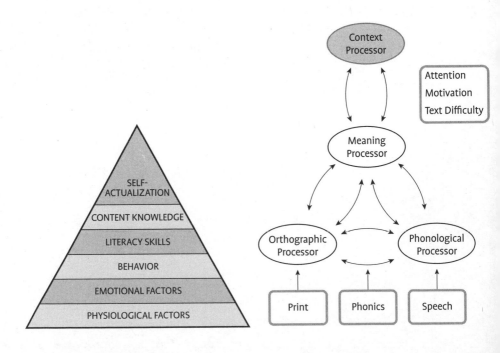

This chapter can help you and your child if:

- ❑ A professional has told you that your child is having reading comprehension difficulty.

- ❑ You've used the Comprehension and Metacognition Checklist in Chapter 4 to determine that your child is having reading comprehension difficulty.

- ❑ Or you're seeing signs that might point to reading comprehension difficulty, such as:

  - Your child has difficulty answering questions about what he is reading.

In this chapter I will:

1. Help you understand the terms *reading comprehension* and *metacognition*.

2. Provide you with ideas that can help you help your child strengthen her reading comprehension and metacognitive skills.

Before you get started on this chapter . . .

Check off all of the following items to make sure that your child's brain is optimally prepared for reading comprehension. **If you can't say "yes" to any item, refer back to Chapter 2.**

- ❑ My child usually eats a diet high in vegetables and fruits and low in processed foods (food packaged in a box or bag that contains more than one ingredient).

- ❑ My child usually gets 8–10 hours of sleep per night.

- ❑ My child usually gets at least 1 hour of vigorous physical activity per day.

- ❑ My child is able to feel, talk about, and appropriately manage a wide range of emotions.

- ❑ My child's behavior usually seems focused and on task.

✦ ✦ ✦

What Are Reading Comprehension and Metacognition?

The term *reading comprehension* means being able to understand what you are reading, and comprehension is the goal of all reading. Reading comprehension is possible when all of the reader's processors—orthographic (visual), phonological (auditory), phonics, meaning (vocabulary), and context (comprehension) (as shown in the PDPM diagram on page 30)—are working well and in coordination with each other. This chapter presents information that you can teach your child to improve his reading comprehension skills, such as the types of reading texts and reading comprehension strategies. Reading comprehension also requires the reader to have adequate attention and motivation and a text that is not too difficult for the reader's skill level. These topics are examined in Chapter 10.

The term *metacognition* refers to a set of self-awareness skills that every reader needs when reading. Readers need to be self-aware (metacognitive) of whether or not they are comprehending what they are reading and what they should do if they realize that comprehension is not taking place. This chapter will teach you how to help your child with these important skills as well.

What Is Text Structure?

One of the first areas to focus on in helping your child improve her reading comprehension is the way in which text is organized, which educators refer to as *text structure*. Understanding text structure is important because it helps children encode the information they are reading. You can think of text structure as a path for navigating text. The more familiar readers are with the path, the easier it will be for them to find their way through the text. There are two primary forms (paths) of text structure: narrative and informational.

Narrative Text

A *narrative* text structure is one that tells a story. To help your child better comprehend narrative texts, discuss the following concepts with your child either during or after reading:

✦ *Setting.* The setting is where the story takes place, and can include the time period, country, state, city, building, and/or room. Some stories take place in multiple settings, and others take place outside, in outer space, under the sea, or in a fantasyland. Reviewing where the story takes place can help your child better comprehend a story.

✦ *Character.* A character is a person, animal, or make-believe individual in the story. The *main character* is the one on which a story primarily focuses. Many stories have one or more characters, and ideally all characters have multifaceted personalities. Helping your child identify and discuss the characters in a story will help him comprehend the story.

✦ *Problem.* In almost all stories, the main character (or characters) has some kind of problem that needs to be solved. Helping your child figure out the problem will help her comprehend the story.

✦ *Goal.* Since almost all stories deal with the resolution of a problem, almost all stories have achieving something as the goal for the main character or characters. Again, helping your child identify the characters' goal will help him better understand the story.

✦ *Plot.* The main events that happen in the story are called the *plot.* Understanding the plot is very important for comprehension.

✦ *Outcome.* The outcome of the story tells how the problem was resolved. Again, to be able to fully comprehend a story, your child will need to understand its outcome.

A great resource for parents who want to help their children better comprehend stories is *Notice and Note: Strategies for Close Reading* (Beers & Probst, 2012). This book, which is extremely popular among educators, teaches readers to look for six key *signposts* when they are reading. These signposts, which I describe briefly next, alert readers that particular information is central to comprehending the story and that they should pay extra close attention. However, to be able to fully integrate these ideas into helping your child overcome reading comprehension difficulty, I suggest that you borrow the book from your local library or purchase your own copy.

✦ *Contrasts and contradictions*. Readers are taught to look for places in the story when something very unexpected happens, such as when a main character thinks or acts in a contradictory way or when something very unusual occurs in the plot or setting

✦ *Tough questions*. Readers are taught to look for a point in the story when characters face a personal, internal struggle or challenge.

✦ *Aha moment*. Readers are taught to look for a point in the story when characters suddenly understand something in a new way.

✦ *Words of the wiser*. Readers are taught to look for a point in the story when words of wisdom are given to the main character or characters.

✦ *Again and again*. Readers are taught to look for words, images, or experiences that repeat throughout the story.

✦ *Memory moment*. Readers are taught to look for places in the text when an important memory, recalled by the main character or characters, often interrupts the flow of the story plot.

Informational Text

In contrast to narrative texts, which tell a story, informational texts convey factual information. Informational texts also have text structures that are different from narrative texts. Helping your child become familiar with these text structures is one of the best ways that you can help her comprehend informational text.

Once your child learns how informational texts are structured, it will be easier for her to comprehend and remember the information that she is reading. Here are the categories of informational text described in *Creating Literacy Instruction for All Students* (Gunning, 2016).

+ *Enumeration—Description.* This type of informational text lists and describes information, such as the ingredients needed for a cookie recipe.

+ *Time Sequence.* This type of informational text is organized around a time sequence, such as a historical chronology.

+ *Explanation—Process.* This type of informational text explains how to do something, such as explaining how to change a flat tire.

+ *Comparison—Contrast.* This type of informational text shows the similarities (comparisons) and differences (contrasts) between concepts, such as religious views.

+ *Problem–Solution.* This type of informational texts explains the relationship between one or more problems and one or more solutions, such as a variety of approaches to helping people save money.

+ *Cause–Effect.* This type of informational text explains the relationship between actions and consequences, such as why certain conditions are a fire hazard.

Just as *Notice and Note: Strategies for Close Reading* (Beers & Probst, 2013) provides signposts for readers to consider, *Literacy Instruction for All Students* (Gunning, 2016) outlines different types of questions that adults can ask children to help them better comprehend the texts that they read. These different kinds of questions will enable your child to better understand what he is reading.

+ *Remember.* Remember questions ask children to recall information exactly as it was presented in the text. For example, what year did the Civil War start?

+ *Understand.* Understand questions ask children to examine relationships between presented concepts. Children are asked to compare, contrast, categorize, and summarize what they have read. Compare questions ask readers to explain the similarities between two or more items, for example, the ways in which the political views of two candidates are the same. Contrast questions ask readers to explain the differences between two or more items, such as the ways in which the political views of two candidates are different. Categorization questions ask children to sort information, for example, sorting items into the categories of solids, liquids, and gases. Summary questions require that readers state the key information from longer pieces of text in an abbreviated form.

✦ *Apply*. Apply questions ask children to use the information in the text to create something new. For example, if a child is reading about the solar system, she may be asked to create a visual representation or three-dimensional model of the solar system.

✦ *Analyze*. Analyze questions ask children to consider the author's purpose and/or point of view in writing the informational text. For example, a child might be asked to consider whether he thinks a text is purely factual or if it was written to be persuasive.

✦ *Evaluate*. Evaluate questions ask children to make a judgment about the quality of a piece of informational text. For example, "Do you feel that the author did a good job explaining how to be a good teammate? Why or why not?"

What Are Comprehension Strategies, and How Can I Teach Them to My Child?

So far in this chapter, I've presented the *concepts* that children need to know to help them comprehend both narrative and informational texts. But knowing the concepts isn't enough. Children also need to master certain *processes* to comprehend what they're reading. Educators call these processes *comprehension strategies*, and they can be grouped into three categories:

✦ Strategies that help readers construct the meaning of a text.

✦ Strategies that help readers monitor whether or not they are comprehending the text.

✦ Fix-up strategies that can be used when readers realize that they are not comprehending the text.

Strategies for Constructing the Meaning of the Text

Reading is an *active process*. At the comprehension level, readers make sense of information at the sentence, paragraph, page, chapter, and book levels. While one part of the reader's brain is actively constructing the meaning of each sentence, another part of the brain is cumulatively building and holding the meaning of sentences, paragraphs, pages, chapters, and books that have already been read. Moreover, the previously read parts of the text can be modified in the reader's mind as he moves forward through the book. For example, a reader may think that a character is kind and generous at the beginning of a book, but later find out that the character also has a sinister side. In other words, the information that the reader already knows about the character is modified in his brain as he continues reading the text.

> *"I found that the best thing to help my daughter's reading comprehension is to have her practice with books that are easy for her. She is able to easily understand these, which really helps her confidence. As her confidence improves, we very slowly move to harder books."*
>
> —Ananya Kaur, mother of a struggling reader

To help readers accomplish the complicated tasks of constructing and remembering the meaning of texts at every level, educational researchers have determined that it's helpful to teach children specific reading comprehension strategies. The five strategies that have been found to be particularly useful in helping readers construct and remember the meaning of the text are described next. *Educational researchers have demonstrated that when children understand and regularly use these strategies, their comprehension of the text improves.*

✦ *Previewing.* In previewing, readers are taught to look through a chapter before reading it. The purpose of previewing is to get the reader's mind ready to absorb new information. When previewing, readers should look to see how long the text is, and whether there are any subsections, headings, illustrations, or definitions of key words.

✦ *Activating prior knowledge.* In activating prior knowledge, readers are taught to think about what they already know about the type of text and the topic before reading. For example, if the text is a mystery, the reader thinks about what she knows about mysteries. If dolphins is the topic of the text, the reader recalls what she already knows about dolphins. Like the strategy of previewing, activating background knowledge helps the reader's mind prepare to absorb the upcoming text.

> *"My son's teacher suggested that my son and I talk a lot about what he is reading when he practices reading at home, so that is what we try to do. We often stop at the end of every paragraph to discuss what is happening in the book. I think this is helping and, hopefully from this practice, he will learn to think about what he is reading when he reads independently."*
>
> —Anthony Mangelli, father of a struggling reader

✦ *Setting a purpose for reading.* Setting a purpose is a third strategy that helps the reader prepare his mind to absorb upcoming information. As the name suggests, this strategy has the reader decide a purpose for reading a paragraph, page, or chapter. For example, in the middle of a book the reader might say to herself, "I'm going to read this chapter to find out what happens next to the main character."

✦ *Predicting.* Predicting is one more strategy that helps the reader prepare his mind to absorb upcoming information. In predicting, the reader makes one or more predictions about what he thinks will happen in the upcoming text and then reads to find out if his prediction was correct.

Strategies for Monitoring Whether or Not Readers Are Comprehending the Text

As one part of a reader's brain actively works to construct a message from the text, a different part of the brain keeps track of whether or not she understands the deciphered message. In other words, a monitoring part of the reader's brain (known as *metacognition*) keeps track of whether or not the reader is understanding the message as she is constructing it during reading. This metacognitive part monitors comprehension along the lines of: "Yes, I understand this. Yes, I understand this. Yes, I understand this. Whoops, I'm confused!" Some readers automatically and intuitively monitor whether or not they are comprehending the messages they are constructing as they read. Other readers, however, need help with strengthening their metacognitive skills. Research has shown that teaching readers how to strengthen their metacognitive skills as they read is one of the most effective ways to improve reading comprehension. Here are two strategies for strengthening metacognition.

> "One way to help your child's reading comprehension is to read with your child and have a conversation about what you read together. It's important to let your child have a choice in the reading material to show that reading is not only for academics, but can be used for entertainment or even as a relaxing activity. Take turns reading parts of the text together so that your child can listen to word pronunciation, your tone, and the emotions you give to the words that are within the text. Then they can pick up on some more reading habits as they listen and watch you read. Pause and ask your child questions as you read together and even invite the child to ask questions as well. Ask what your child notices and wonders as the child reads the text with you. Reading together can spark a conversation that can give you plenty of insight as to what your child is comprehending in a text."
>
> —Jiana Marie DeJesus, seventh-grade language arts teacher and reading specialist

✦ *Visualizing.* In visualizing, readers form a picture in their mind of what is happening in the text during or immediately after reading. Children can be coached to repeatedly read and then visualize as they take in information. For example, you could say, "This passage describes things you can do at home on a rainy day. Can you close your eyes and tell me what you see in your mind's eye as you think about this?" If your child can't describe a picture of what is happening in the text, it is usually a clue that she is not understanding what she is reading.

✦ *Summarizing.* Summarizing is a classic strategy for helping readers coalesce their understanding of a text. When summarizing, children are asked to recall the central ideas of a paragraph, page, chapter, or book that they have just read. Similar to visualizing, if your child can't summarize what he has just read, it is usually a clue that he is not adequately understanding it. To help your child learn to summarize, start with a single paragraph. As you read through the paragraph, discuss whether each sentence is a main idea or a supporting detail. Then repeat the process with another paragraph and then a third. A summary of the three paragraphs should include the main idea from each one. As your child progresses with this skill, more paragraphs can be included. Some paragraphs contain only supporting details and do not need to be reflected in summaries.

Fix-up Strategies That Help When Readers Realize They Are Not Understanding What They're Reading

As I've just described, the metacognitive part of a reader's brain monitors comprehension as the reader constructs meaning from the text. When readers reach a "Whoops, I'm confused" part of a text, they need to employ one or more *fix-up strategies* to get back on track:

✦ *Reread.* A great strategy for your child to use when he realizes he's not comprehending the text is to read the material again. Your child can go back as far as is necessary to ensure that comprehension is occurring.

✦ *Slow down.* Another fix-up strategy to aid comprehension is to slow your child's reading pace. Be sure your child is reading slowly enough to understand what she's reading. Slowing the reading pace is particularly effective when combined with rereading.

✦ *Reorient.* Reorienting means that the reader pulls back his attention from the immediate sentence or paragraph to review the larger context of the text. In reading narrative text, the reader may look at chapter titles and/or illustrations to remind himself of what is happening in the book. In reading informational text, the reader may also look at chapter subheadings.

✦ *Look up a word.* Sometimes it's the meaning of a single word or a few words that prevent a child from understanding what she's reading. When this happens, help your child learn how to look up the meanings of unknown words.

> *"One thing I have learned from working with students over the years is to never forget the collaborative nature of learning. Socialization during the reading process facilitates deeper understanding and the discovery of nuances of the text and its meaning, as well as heightened enjoyment. It is for this reason that many adults join book clubs. For children it is even more important to have someone with whom to thoughtfully discuss worthy texts. If you read what your child is reading, and pose thoughtful questions, talk about what is interesting to you or what moved you, it will motivate your child to dig deeper into his or her own understanding. Share joy at the use of a word or a turn of phrase. This will help build your child's vocabulary, which has a direct impact on reading comprehension. Reread interesting parts of the text and share any connections to you or your child's personal life. Both of you can visit the library or bookstore together to choose a book with a topic or theme that interests you both. Start your own private book club, and make it fun!"*
>
> —Eileen Schwebel, certified reading specialist
> and supervisor of English language arts

✦ *Ask for help.* It's important to teach your child to ask for help if she is really struggling with a reading task. Children should not "just keep reading" if understanding is not taking place. When children ask parents or teachers for help, adults learn what areas need attention. This awareness enables us to provide the most supportive, individualized instruction possible for them.

✦ *Take a break.* Last, sometimes children just need to take a break and come back to reading at another time. Reading can be very hard work for children, and knowing when to take a break is an important fix-up strategy when comprehension suffers.

How Can I Teach My Child Comprehension Strategies?

I recommend the following sequence of instructional steps for teaching comprehension strategies. I've used the example of teaching the process or strategy of previewing a text before reading it to illustrate how to teach this strategy.

✦ *Introduce.* First, introduce the strategy to your child. You can say something like "Today, I'm going to teach you how to preview a text. Previewing a text means looking through the text to get familiar with it."

✦ *Demonstrate.* After introducing the strategy in words, show your child how to implement the strategy. In the example of previewing, show your child how you look through the text to get familiar with it. It will probably be helpful to your child if you *think aloud* as you preview. For example, you can say something like "I see that this chapter is 10 pages long and is divided into three different parts. I also see that there are three illustrations and a summary section at the end."

> "When teaching literacy, a major goal is to get students to have thoughts and wonderings about what they read. Giving children sticky notes to jot down their questions, thoughts, and wonderings is a great way to get them to think about what they are reading. Getting children to think about why the character is acting the way he or she is acting, or why the problem was solved the way it was solved, or simply why the setting takes place where it does gets kids thinking about text! This aids immensely in their comprehension of fiction text."
>
> —Bettina Bergamo, fifth-grade teacher

✦ *Shared practice.* In shared practice, you and your child practice the strategy together. For the previewing example, you can select several different portions of the text and together become familiar with them. Be sure to talk about the strategy as you are practicing it together.

✦ *Independent practice.* After you have introduced and demonstrated the strategy, and after you and your child have practiced using it together, it is time for your child to practice using the strategy independently. I suggest giving your child easy text to practice the strategy at first. As your child gets more proficient using the strategy, more difficult reading texts can be introduced.

What Is Guided Reading, and How Can I Implement It at Home?

So far in this chapter, I've provided a description of the two primary kinds of texts with which children need to be familiar (narrative and informational), a variety of reading comprehension strategies that children need to be able to use, and a sequence of steps through which you can teach these comprehension strategies to your child. In this section, I'll explain how to put together a complete reading comprehension lesson for your child. Educators refer to this type of lesson as *guided reading* because adults use it to guide children in learning how to read with comprehension.

How Can I Implement Guided Reading at Home?

Think of guided reading lessons as consisting of three parts: *before reading*, *during reading*, and *after reading*.

In the *before-reading* part of your guided reading lesson, prepare your child to read by:

+ Introducing the selected text

+ Highlighting a few key vocabulary words from the text

+ Teaching (or reviewing) one of the concepts, skills, or strategies previously described to apply during the lesson.

For example, you might say, "Today we're going to begin reading an informational book about turtles, and we're going to focus on the reading strategy of visualizing." Then review the format of the informational book, identify and discuss five (or so) important vocabulary words in the book, and review the visualizing reading strategy. As a general guideline, the *before-reading* part of a guided reading lesson should take about 10 minutes.

In the *during-reading* part of your guided reading lesson, have your child read aloud the selected text to you or, if your child prefers, take turns reading it aloud. You can also have your child silently read the text to herself during this part of the lesson. Regardless of how the text is read, be sure to discuss your previously identified key vocabulary words as you come across them during reading and also to have your child practice using the day's target concept or reading strategy. The during-reading part of the guided reading lesson should take between 10 and 30 minutes, depending on your child's age, with younger children having shorter reading sessions.

In the *after-reading* part of the lesson, again review the day's key vocabulary words and reading concept or strategy. Then add an after-reading comprehension activity. Depending on your child's age, after-reading comprehension activities can include summarizing the text, answering written questions, or making creative artistic responses to the text. The after-reading part is also age dependent and should take between 5 and 20 minutes.

Chapter Highlights

Reading comprehension—understanding what you're reading—is the goal of all reading, and it's possible when all of the readers' processors—visual, auditory, phonics, vocabulary, and comprehension—are working well and in coordination with each other. To improve reading comprehension skills, your child needs to know the different types of reading texts and to learn a variety of reading comprehension strategies. Readers also need to develop *metacognition,* a set of self-awareness skills, to know whether they're comprehending what they're reading and what to do if they are not. Research studies have shown that the strategies presented in this chapter can boost your child's reading comprehension.

10

What Should I Do If My Child Is Having Difficulty with Attention and/or Motivation?

I have no special talent. I am only passionately curious.

—ALBERT EINSTEIN (overcame reading
difficulty to become a scientist)

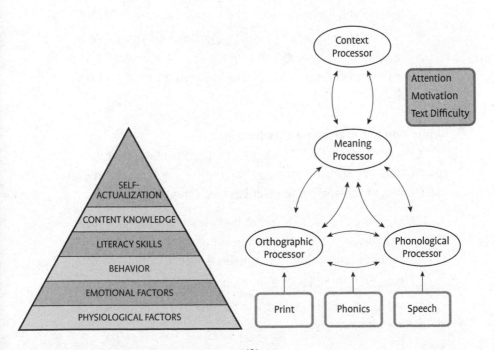

This chapter can help you and your child if:

❏ A professional has told you that your child is having difficulty with attention or motivation.

❏ You've used the Attention and Motivation Checklists in Chapter 4 to determine that your child is having difficulty with attention and/or motivation.

❏ Or you're seeing signs that might point to attention or motivation difficulty, such as:

- Your child has difficulty focusing on what he is reading and/or does not want to read.

In this chapter I will:

1. Explain the concept of *text difficulty* and its role in reading achievement and help you learn how to find the right level of texts for your child to read.

2. Explain the concept of *attention* and its role in reading achievement and provide you with activities and resources to help you improve your child's ability to pay attention.

3. Explain the concept of reading *motivation* and its role in reading achievement and provide you with activities and resources to help you increase your child's motivation to read.

Before you get started on this chapter . . .

Check off all of the following items to make sure that your child's brain is optimally prepared for auditory processing. **If you can't say "yes" to any item, refer back to Chapter 2.**

❏ My child usually eats a diet high in vegetables and fruits and low in processed foods (food packaged in a box or bag that contains more than one ingredient).

❏ My child usually gets 8–10 hours of sleep per night.

❏ My child usually gets at least 1 hour of vigorous physical activity per day.

❑ My child is able to feel, talk about, and appropriately manage a wide range of emotions.

❑ My child's behavior usually seems focused and on task.

✦ ✦ ✦

Attention, Motivation, and Text Difficulty

Before you can fully understand attention and motivation related to reading, it's important to understand the concept of text difficulty. *Text difficulty* is a measure of how easy or hard any given text is to read, which can obviously affect a child's motivation to read and ability to pay attention while reading.

Text Difficulty

What Is Text Difficulty, and Why Is It Important?

Most book publishers assign a *text difficulty level* to books and online reading materials when they market them. Text difficulty levels help educators, librarians, and parents determine whether a text is too easy, too difficult, or just right for any individual child. You can think of a text's difficulty level as being similar to a *shoe size* for sports. If you want your child to do a great job playing soccer, basketball, or baseball, you'll need to buy athletic shoes that fit perfectly. The same is true for reading. If you want your child to do a great job with reading, you'll need to make sure that the texts you're giving him are the ideal fit for his level of skill. Be careful not to just use your child's grade level when selecting reading material. That would be like assuming that shoes between a size 4 and a size 6 should work for your child because most kids his age wear these sizes. There is a wide range of individual variations in children's reading ability levels within the same grade. To optimize your child's reading success, I strongly suggest that you take some time to learn your child's reading level and how to match his reading level with the difficulty of the texts that you select for him to read. Information on how to tackle these important tasks is presented in the sections that follow.

How Can I Figure Out My Child's Reading Level and Find Books at the "Right" Level of Difficulty for Her?

Just as the sales assistant who works in a shoe store needs to measure your child's foot to make sure that her new gym shoes will fit well, you need to measure your child's reading ability to find texts that are at the right level of difficulty for her to read. If the books that you choose are too hard for her, she will likely have trouble with reading comprehension, attention, and motivation. If the books that you choose are too easy for her, she will likely get bored, and her reading practice will not help her grow as a reader. The section "Monitoring Your Child's Reading Level" in Chapter 4 can help you learn how to measure your child's level of reading skill.

> *"My son loves when I read to him. He loves the* Harry Potter *books in particular. These books are much too hard for him to read by himself, but when I read them to him, he really pays attention. Then we talk about them. I think that reading books together is the best way to help him become a good reader and a person who loves reading."*
> —Martin Templeton, father of a struggling reader

Once you've determined your child's reading level, you can search the Internet for books and other reading materials that match that level. Keep in mind that these reading materials are labeled using grade numbers that relate specifically to text difficulty, not to the grade your child is in at school. So if your child is in the third grade, but her reading skill level is at grade 2, you would search online for "grade 2 books," not "grade 3 books."

This search will yield hundreds, if not thousands, of books that will be ideally matched for your child's stage of reading development. But if you need more, these websites are terrific sources for locating texts exactly at your child's reading level:

✦ Newsela.com. This website offers current news stories, written for children's consumption, at varying levels of text difficulty. For example, your child might be interested in a current political election or a recent scientific discovery. You and your child can search the site for the news item and then choose to read the news story at the right level of text difficulty for your child.

✦ ReadingA-Z.com. This website offers fiction and nonfiction books at a variety of text levels. Simply choose your child's text level, and a long list of choices will appear.

Attention

What Is Attention, and Why Is It Important in Reading?

Attention is the ability to concentrate on the task at hand. As explained in earlier chapters, reading is composed of many subskills (identifying letters, processing sounds, matching letters with sounds, attaching vocabulary meaning, constructing the meaning of the text, monitoring whether or not text comprehension is occurring, and using fix-up strategies). Attention difficulty will make mastery of these tasks much harder.

What Causes Attention Difficulty?

Attention problems are caused by a variety of factors. If you've ruled out problems with the foundational factors noted at the beginning of this chapter, consider other possible causes:

✦ Environmental distractions and discomforts

✦ Motivational problems

✦ Text difficulty

✦ Chemical imbalances in the brain

Chapter 4 can help you identify the factor or factors that may be causing attention difficulty for your child. If environmental distractions or lack of motivation seem to be contributing to attention problems, you can tweak your child's environment to enhance attention as described in the next section. If you've measured your child's reading skill level and found that he is reading material that is too hard or too easy, you can first seek out reading materials at the appropriate level of text difficulty as I've just discussed. Motivation and its relation to attention are discussed later in this chapter. If you've ruled out these three factors, it's possible that your child has a chemical imbalance in the brain. Your school district or pediatrician can refer your child for an evaluation for a chemical imbalance that is causing attention problems and, if indicated, medication can be prescribed. *It is my firm belief that medication for an attention problem should not be prescribed unless all of the preceding potential sources of attention difficulty have been investigated and addressed. If a full investigation confirms that your child needs medication for an attention problem then, by all means, the proper medication should be prescribed and taken.*

"The influence of reading to a child or even having children see a family member sit down and read is monumental, no matter the age of the child. Children want to explore the world around them, and showing a child how to read can introduce an entirely new realm of discovery. I would encourage all family members to read to the children in the family. Read to children while they are in the womb, when they are tiny, snuggled-up newborns, when they are little toddlers touching and grabbing everything in sight, and even when they can read themselves. Children pick up on family members' habits, so read to them. Let them see every family member read a book or a magazine. You may be surprised when one day your child flips through the pages of a book rather than plays with all of the toys scattered everywhere."

—Jiana Marie DeJesus, seventh-grade language arts teacher and reading specialist

Creating an Environment That Will Help Your Child Focus

One important aspect of helping your child with attention is creating an environment that helps her focus. This begins with planning, which ideally can be completed collaboratively. In the planning stage, you and your child need to address the factors related to the physical environment of your home and to the timing aspects of her reading.

Every child needs a space at home that is well suited for reading. This space should be physically comfortable, well lit, quiet, and, as much as possible, free from distractions, such as people nearby. In some homes, the best place for a child to read is in her bed. In other homes, there may be a sofa or cozy chair that is just right for curling up with a book. Some children like beanbag chairs or child-size, cartooned-themed furniture. Regardless of how you and your child create her reading space, make sure that it appeals to her and that she consistently uses it when reading.

After your child's physical reading space has been created, you both need to agree on timing parameters:

+ How often will your child read?

+ For how long will your child read?

+ When will your child read?

Ideally, children should read every day, but in some families skipping 1 or 2 days per week may be unavoidable because of family schedules. What is more important is that first you and your child agree on how many days a week he will read. Then you need to agree on the length of time devoted to reading each day. Be realistic about what is appropriate for your child's level of development; in general, the younger the child, the shorter the reading session should be. It is also a good idea to set aside time each day for reading to and with your child and for your child to read independently. As an example, if your child is in third grade, each evening you might read *with* your child for 10 minutes and then read *to* your child for 10 more minutes. Last, you might ask your child to read *independently* for 10 minutes. Ideally, you and your child will agree to a schedule that works for your whole family and will be consistent about implementing the plan.

Activities for Strengthening Attention

In addition to these guidelines, the following activities may be helpful in strengthening your child's ability to focus. Because research clearly indicates that children attend best when tasks interest them, these activities have built-in appeal for children.

+ *Board games.* Playing board games with your child is a great way to strengthen his attention. For young children, try Candy Land, Chutes and Ladders, and Memory. For older children, try Monopoly, chess, and backgammon.

✦ *Puzzles.* Doing puzzles with your child will also improve her attention. Puzzles come in a variety of types and are designed for children at different developmental levels. Enjoy this calming and engaging activity together!

✦ *Building activities.* Building activities will also strengthen your child's ability to pay attention. Lego kits, in which children need to follow step-by-step directions, are famous for keeping children spellbound. Other building activities focus on model cars, boats, and airplanes, or free-form building, such as with K'NEX, building blocks, or magnetic tiles.

There are also many electronic resources that help children improve their attention skill. A few recommended websites are:

✦ Mentalup.co. This website provides mind and brain activities designed to help children strengthen their mental skills.

✦ Lumosity.com. Originally created to help adults sharpen their cognitive skills, this website now has brain-strengthening activities for children.

✦ Headspace.com. This free online application is dedicated to helping people learn and practice mindfulness meditation. Mindfulness meditation has been shown to increase children's, adolescents', and adults' ability to focus and pay attention. Meditation has also been linked to physical and emotional health benefits, such as decreased stress levels and an increased sense of peace and well-being.

Motivation

What Is Motivation?

In general, motivation refers to a person's desire or willingness to participate in a particular activity. When educators discuss children's motivation to read, they think about how interested the child is in reading, how dedicated the child is to improving her reading ability, and how much confidence the child has in her ability to read and to grow as a reader. Educators and psychologists also acknowledge that there are two kinds of motivation: extrinsic and intrinsic. *Extrinsic motivation* occurs when a task is completed to get some kind of external reward, such as a sticker, a treat, or money. *Intrinsic motivation* occurs when a task is completed because the person experiences great joy or satisfaction in engaging in the task. Helping children become intrinsically motivated readers is the optimal goal of reading educators; however, both educators and parents may need to use extrinsic rewards to gradually help children's behavior move in the direction of intrinsic motivation.

How Is Motivation Related to Reading Achievement?

Motivation is central to reading achievement because motivated readers read much more than unmotivated readers. Each time a reader reads, he gets better and better at the activity. Conversely, the less a reader reads, the less his skills get strengthened. Research has indicated that motivated readers read significantly more often, and for longer periods of time, than do reluctant readers. When one considers the cumulative impact of such differences year after year, it is easy to see how motivated readers become high-achievement readers, and reluctant readers often become low-achievement readers. The following guidelines and activities can help you help your child become an intrinsically motivated reader.

Guidelines to Strengthen Reading Motivation

John Guthrie is arguably the most famous educator in the field of children's reading motivation. He spent his entire career as a professor at the University of Maryland, winning many prestigious research and federally funded grant awards for his work. Here is a summary of his key recommendations for facilitating children's reading motivation, along with activity suggestions.

✦ *Relevance.* Choosing reading materials that are relevant and of interest to children's lives is probably the best-known way to improve reading motivation. Does your child have a particular interest—perhaps in a sport or professional performer? Find reading materials on that subject. Even topics such as video gaming, skateboarding, and the *Jurassic World* adventure film have texts written about them. Finding reading materials on topics that interest your child (and of course are at the appropriate level of difficulty) is one of the most important factors in motivating children to read.

✦ *Choice.* Research indicates that choice is another factor that is closely linked to reading motivation; as choice increases, so does a child's motivation to read. Give your child choices about what to read and about what kind of activities are done before and after reading to strengthen reading skills.

✦ *Success.* Success is a third factor that is closely linked to reading motivation; the more success that your child has with reading, the greater his motivation to read will be. As discussed earlier in this chapter, experiencing success is one of the primary reasons that picking texts that are not too difficult for your child is so important.

✦ *Social collaboration.* Guthrie's research was primarily conducted in school settings where he found that children working together (social collaboration) was a fourth factor closely linked to reading motivation; as children experienced increased opportunities for social collaboration during reading, their motivation to read increased. In applying this research finding to a home setting, you may notice that giving your child the opportunity to take turns reading with a sibling, cousin, or friend will be motivating. Children can take turns reading the pages of a shared book out loud to each other.

✦ *Emphasizing the importance of reading.* Guthrie also found that in school settings it was extremely important for teachers to continually remind their students that becoming proficient readers was the goal of reading. At home, continue to remind your child of the importance of reading as well. Point out to your child that one reason for becoming a proficient reader is that, once she knows how to read well, she can read and learn about anything in the world in which she is interested!

✦ *Thematic units of study.* The concept of thematic units of study refers to the studying of items that are connected to each other. As in the other motivation ideas I've listed, Guthrie's research showed that when children read about topics that were connected to each other, their motivation to read increased. For example, if your child loves fishing, his motivation to read will increase if he reads about the many different aspects of fish and fishing, such as types of fish and their habitats, best fishing practices, and stories about famous fishers.

> "To help intrinsically motivate children to read, I suggest making the experience interest based, fun, and real to a reader's life. Taking your child to a bookstore, spending time browsing the shelves, reading the back covers of books together, and discussing what the books are about are great ways to model a reader's strategy to self-select books. Having your children know how to select a book that interests them is crucial to building foundational reading habits."
>
> —Peggy Schaneman, reading specialist

✦ *Adult–child relationships.* Guthrie's research in school settings indicated that the quality of the teacher–student relationship was closely related to motivation to read. In other words, the better the relationship between the teacher and the student, the higher the student's motivation to read. This finding is likely applicable to parent–child relationships as well.

It is also worth mentioning that Guthrie found that the following factors *decreased* reading motivation: (1) negative feedback to a child, such as excessive corrections, scolding, or shaming; (2) removal of choice; (3) texts that were too difficult for the child to read with ease; and (4) texts that did not interest the child.

Activities to Strengthen Reading Motivation

In addition to these general guidelines for increasing motivation, consider trying the following fun reading and writing activities to boost your child's motivation to read:

✦ *Zoom pajama reading.* Does your child have a favorite relative or friend? Consider putting on pajamas and having a nighttime Zoom pajama reading time!

✦ *Reading to animals.* Does your child love animals? Pets often love having children read to them. If you don't have your own pet, animal shelters will often let volunteers visit and read to their dogs and cats. Apparently dogs will calm down and listen when children read to them.

> "It might sound strange to say, but I realized that it was my responsibility to help my daughter a lot at home. When she first started school, I always thought that it was the school's responsibility to teach her to read. I still think that's true, but now I understand that my daughter is just one of those kids who needs me to help her a lot at home too."
> —Jennifer Hu, mother of a struggling reader

✦ *Reading recipes, cooking, and baking.* Do you and your child enjoy cooking and baking together? Creating a shopping list, shopping for ingredients, and reading a recipe are full of literacy-building opportunities.

✦ *Writing to authors, illustrators, and other famous individuals.* Does your child have a favorite author, illustrator, or other famous person? Consider sending a card, letter, or email to him or her. Very often your child will get a response. Writing to the famous person will be educational; receiving a response will be thrilling!

✦ *Writing to community leaders.* Does your child have strong opinions on social issues related to your community, state, or country? Perhaps she wants a bike lane so she can bike to school or to have a weekly farmers' market, a community garden, a playground, or a skate park nearby? Encourage your child to write to community leaders. Again, she will often receive a reply, which will be motivating, and sometimes the expressed desire will be fulfilled!

I also recommend the following online resources to improve reading motivation:

✦ Storylineonline.net. On this website, famous actors, sports figures, authors, illustrators, and other celebrities post videos of themselves reading stories to children. Tune in to find your favorite celebrity reading aloud a great book!

✦ Uniteforliteracy.com. Unite for Literacy is a remarkable online resource especially devoted to children for whom English is not their first language. The site hosts dozens of picture books that can be viewed and listened to in 50 different languages. A sign language version is also available. The audiobook is "read" first in the selected language and then in English. Check this site out with your child. You won't be disappointed—it's amazing!

✦ Kids.nationalgeographic.com. This motivating website is devoted to helping children learn about the world in enjoyable and interesting ways. Browse through for educational and engaging videos, games, and reading resources.

Chapter Highlights

This chapter addresses the topics of text difficulty, attention, and motivation in reading. The three topics are closely related and interwoven because, if children's texts are too difficult for them to read with ease, they will not have enough internal attention to construct the meaning of what they are reading. Not only will an overly difficult text interfere with reading comprehension, it will also lower children's motivation to read. Therefore, you need to determine your child's reading level and then find texts that are well suited for that level. Be sure to check your child's reading level at the beginning of each new school marking period (see Chapter 4). This chapter also provides information on how to help your child improve her ability to pay attention during reading and how to improve her motivation to read.

A Few Final Words
Putting It All Together

As you reach the final few pages of this book, I'd like to congratulate you on your hard work and perseverance. As I stated at the start of the first chapter, for most of us, modern life is complicated, demanding, and often overwhelming. Raising children is a long-term and serious responsibility, and raising a child who has a reading difficulty makes that job even harder. Congratulations to you and your family for setting aside the time, and doing the work, of addressing reading difficulty. Truly, I understand how hard this can be, and I commend you on your efforts and progress.

I'd also like to thank you for trusting me to guide you through the process of learning how to help your child overcome reading difficulty. As a professional educator and psychotherapist, I have dedicated my life to learning how to help children cognitively and emotionally. It gives me great satisfaction to know that my hard work is being passed along and put to good use by parents and their children.

What You Have Learned

In this book, I've tried to provide you with the key elements of learning how to help your child overcome reading difficulty. This endeavor was accomplished in three ways. First, I helped you learn about the reading process itself and the many factors that contribute to reading success. Second, I provided checklists to help you determine which factors may be causing your child's reading difficulty. Third, I offered information about how to provide targeted intervention and support for each area of your child's challenge.

One way to reflect on what you've mastered (or haven't yet mastered!) is to consider the following questions. Feel free to write your answers in the space provided:

1. What are the most important things my child and I have learned reading this book?

2. What are the areas in which my child and I have made progress as a result of this book?

3. What are the areas in which my child and I still need to do more work?

4. How has my understanding of the reading process changed as a result of reading this book?

5. How has my understanding of the factors contributing to my child's reading difficulty changed as a result of reading this book?

6. How has my ability to help my child overcome reading difficulty changed as a result of reading this book?

7. What areas still concern me most about my child's reading?

8. Do I feel that I need to seek professional support to further help my child?

What You've Gained

As you reflect back on what you learned as a result of reading this book, I also invite you to consider the benefits you've gained beyond increased reading-specific knowledge. For example, I'm hoping that your confidence about your ability to help your child has grown and that your stress level regarding not knowing how to help your child has decreased. Also, is there now less conflict between you and other family members as a result of your child's improved reading? And is there more joy now around reading? All of these gains are additional benefits to you and your family as a result of your understanding and applying the information in this book.

Ideally, your child will have been the primary recipient of benefits from your use and application of this book. In addition to an improved physiological foundation, which strengthens brain function, and stronger visual processing, auditory processing, phonics skills, vocabulary, comprehension, attention, and motivation, I hope that your child is also now experiencing less stress and conflict and more overall happiness. As these widespread benefits are felt and absorbed, your child may find a continually expanding circle of positive effects associated with his improved reading. These positive changes often include improved school performance, improved sibling and peer relationships, and improved confidence, self-esteem, and self-image.

Looking at the literacy pyramid one last time, we can see that another benefit of improved reading skill for your child is greater access to the content knowledge in which she is interested. Content knowledge

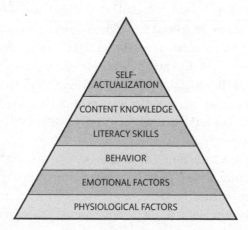

refers to the information that we all need to know to choreograph the life that we want to live. Perhaps your child wants to be a veterinarian, an artist, a real estate developer, or a farmer. All of these careers require the mastery of content knowledge. In addition, there is the need to be an informed citizen, an educated consumer, and a financially literate person. Many of us also seek to be the best that we can be in our social relationships and in our roles as partners, parents, siblings, children, friends, employees, colleagues, and so on. All of these pursuits require content knowledge, which is primarily accessible when one has adequate reading skills.

Helping our children decide which area or areas of content knowledge they want to focus on as they begin to choreograph their lives is also critical. The cornerstone of helping children do this is helping them become aware of their own areas of interest and their varying levels of curiosity about different content knowledge areas. Perhaps your child loves sports, as many do. Can you help her pursue one sport each season? Might her love of sports grow into a career? Other children may enjoy hiking, biking, cooking, dance, music, animals, gardening, or cars. As much as possible, foster and support your child's desire to learn about and engage in activities that relate to her interests.

Some children seem to gravitate only to video games and/or enjoy them the most. Can they take computer classes and learn how to create their own electronic games? For children who enjoy only being in electronic environments, I do suggest setting time limits. Perhaps your child can be in the virtual world for an hour each day after he has completed his homework, chores, and other daily responsibilities. While electronic environments can be beneficial to children's development in some ways, too often they have an addictive quality and are a way to avoid being fully engaged with life. I am also an advocate of reducing television time, for the same reasons. In general, I believe in turning off electronics as much as possible and connecting to other aspects of ourselves that provide our bodies and minds with the nourishment and challenges they need to create the lives that we want.

Using the literacy pyramid as a guide, we can see that when individuals take good care of their physiological, emotional, behavioral, literacy, and content knowledge needs, a self-actualized life is attainable. This means that when individuals take good care of these important needs, they can live the lives that they really want. Throughout this book, I have included quotations from famous world figures who have overcome reading challenges and built self-actualized lives. In closing, I share the story of one mother, her son who experienced reading difficulty, and his pursuit of a self-actualized life.

Mrs. Mary Ann Gasper (52) describing her experience with her son, Joseph (18), a struggling reader

I realized that Joseph had a reading problem in the second half of fifth grade. When Joseph was younger, we always had a literacy-rich home where we read books with our children, and it seemed like both of my sons enjoyed reading and being read to. At that time, Joseph went to Catholic school, and his classes had about 30 students in each room. The school didn't send home much of Joseph's work but, as far as I could tell, he was doing well.

Then when Joseph was starting fifth grade, my husband and I decided to transfer him to a public school. The public school sent work home. Some of it was work that he had completed at school, and some of it was reading and writing that he needed to complete at home. That's when I started to notice that he was having difficulty reading. Sometimes he would substitute words for other words. Other times, he would just completely make up something. I remember being in denial about what was happening. Denial is really the right word. He was really struggling, but I had trouble realizing it. Finally, one day, and I will never forget this [becoming emotional], I said to him "just read what's on the page," and he replied, "Mom, the words are dancing on the page." I'll never forget that.

After Joseph told me that, I immediately took him to the eye doctor, thinking that he had a vision problem. He did need glasses for a minor correction, but that was not what was making the words dance on the page. Finally, it became clear to me that there was some other kind of problem. By then, Joseph was 11 and, in addition to his reading difficulty, he had a lack of self-esteem. There was no way that I was going to put him through a child-study team evaluation at his new school, and there were no records from the Catholic school that indicated he had any learning difficulties. Instead my husband and I decided to ask a friend of ours who is a special education teacher to test him. When she was done with the testing, she told us that Joseph has dyslexia. She also created a 504 plan for him that allows him to have special accommodations in school and for standardized testing.

When Joseph was diagnosed with dyslexia in the second half of fifth grade, I started beating myself up. I really wanted to kick myself. I couldn't believe that I hadn't seen the signs earlier. I had really been in denial.

Although I was beating myself up, Joseph was very accepting of the diagnosis. Maybe he was relieved to know that there was a reason that reading had been so hard for him. Also, once we understood the problem, we were able to start finding strategies to help him. Joseph has difficulty reading when black ink is used on white paper; that is when the letters "dance." I realized this when I noticed that his notebook had very little writing in it but instead was filled with a variety of different colored Post-it notes. He explained to me that he sees print better when it is on colored paper. Knowing that he can read much better when black ink is on colored paper, I started buying reams of colored paper and offering them to his teachers. His teachers were great about this, and never objected to creating special copies for Joseph so that he could read them more easily. The teachers also sent PowerPoint slides home for him for extra help, and we found online websites that supported his learning, such as Learning Ally, where he could listen to books rather than having to read them.

By the time that Joseph graduated high-school, he had a 3.9 GPA and had become an Eagle Scout. He had also earned six scholarships for college, and had 12 credits from the local community college through a collaborative program, with a 4.0 GPA. Joseph had his heart set on attending a selective engineering university but, unfortunately, despite all of his accomplishments, he was initially rejected because he doesn't test well. At first, Joseph felt defeated, as attending this particular school was his dream. Quickly, however, his resilience returned. He retook the SATs, met with representatives of the university on two occasions, and created a portfolio of his work with his guidance counselor. Finally, Joseph was accepted to the university of his dreams.

As we can see from this moving testament, reading difficulty can be overcome and self-actualized lives can be realized following reading challenges. Improved reading skills will open doors to the content knowledge that your child wants, enabling her to fulfill her potential. Improved reading skills will raise your child's self-confidence, self-esteem, and self-image. Improved reading skills will stimulate your child's imagination, free his mind, and multiply his choices throughout life. Your hard work in reading and applying the information in this book has, and always will have, lifelong benefits. I wish you and your child the greatest lives possible, and that all of your dreams come true.

Appendix

Word Family
and Sight-Word Lists

Both lists in this appendix are reprinted from *The Reading Teacher's Book of Lists* (Jacqueline E. Kress & Edward B. Fry, 2015).

Word Families   **155**

Sight Words   **165**

Word Families

Phonograms, or rimes, have been used in the teaching of reading since colonial times and continue to be an instructional mainstay in regular classrooms, remedial and corrective reading instruction, English as a second language classes, and adult literacy instruction. The phonograms in this comprehensive list are all one-syllable words; however, the same phonograms appear in many polysyllabic words. Use these patterned words for phonics practice and spelling.

-ab /a/	-ack /a/	dad	-aft /a/	-age /ā/	snail	lair	flake
cab	back	fad	daft	cage	trail	pair	shake
dab	hack	gad	raft	gage		chair	snake
gab	Jack	had	waft	page	-ain	flair	stake
jab	lack	lad	craft	rage	/ā/	stair	
lab	Mack	mad	draft	sage	lain		-ale
nab	pack	pad	graft	wage	main	-aise	/ā/
tab	quack	sad	shaft	stage	pain	/ā/	bale
blab	rack	tad			rain	raise	dale
crab	sack	Brad		-aid	vain	braise	gale
drab	tack	Chad	-ag	/ā/	wain	chaise	hale
flab	black	clad	/a/	laid	brain	praise	male
grab	clack	glad	bag	maid	chain		pale
scab	crack	shad	gag	paid	drain	-ait	sale
slab	knack		hag	raid	grain	/ā/	tale
stab	shack	-ade	jag	braid	plain	bait	scale
	slack	/ā/	lag	staid	slain	gait	shale
	smack	bade	nag		Spain	wait	stale
	snack	fade	rag	-ail	sprain	strait	whale
	stack	jade	sag	/ā/	stain	trait	
	track	made	tag	bail	strain		-alk
-ace	whack	wade	wag	fail	train	-ake	/aw/
/ā/		blade	brag	Gail		/ā/	balk
face	-act	glade	crag	hail	-aint	bake	calk
lace	/a/	grade	drag	jail	/ā/	cake	talk
mace	fact	shade	flag	mail	faint	fake	walk
pace	pact	spade	shag	nail	paint	Jake	chalk
race	tact	trade	slag	pail	saint	lake	stalk
brace	tract		snag	quail	taint	make	
grace		-aff	stag	rail	quaint	quake	-all
place	-ad	/a/	swag	sail		rake	/ô/
space	/a/	gaff		tail	-air	take	ball
trace	bad	chaff		wail	/air/	wake	call
	cad	quaff		flail	fair	brake	fall
		staff			hair	drake	gall

155

hall
mall
pall
tall
wall
small
squall
stall

-alt
/aw/
halt
malt
salt

-am
/a/
cam
dam
ham
jam
Pam
ram
Sam
tam
yam
clam
cram
dram
gram
scam
scram
sham
slam
swam
tram

-ame
/ā/
came
dame
fame
game
lame
name
same
tame

blame
flame
frame
shame

-amp
/a/
camp
damp
lamp
ramp
tamp
vamp
champ
clamp
cramp
scamp
stamp
tramp

-an
/a/
ban
can
Dan
fan
man
pan
ran
van
bran
clan
flan
plan
scan
span
than

-ance
/a/
dance
lance
chance
France
glance
prance

stance
trance
twang

-anch
/a/
ranch
blanch
branch
stanch

-and
/a/
band
hand
land
sand
bland
brand
gland
stand
strand

-ane
/ā/
bane
cane
Jane
lane
mane
pane
sane
vane
wane
crane
plane

-ang
/ā/
bang
fang
gang
hang
pang
rang
sang
tang
clang

slang
sprang
twang

-ank
/ā/
bank
dank
hank
lank
rank
sank
tank
yank
blank
clank
crank
drank
flank
Frank
plank
prank
shank
stank
thank

-ant
/a/
can't
pant
rant
chant
grant
plant
scant
slant

-ap
/a/
cap
gap
lap
map
nap
pap
rap
sap

tap
yap
chap
clap
flap
scrap
slap
snap
strap
trap
wrap

-ape
/ā/
cape
gape
nape
rape
tape
drape
grape
scrape
shape

-ar
/ar/
bar
car
far
jar
mar
par
tar
char
scar
spar
star

-ard
/ar/
bard
card
guard
hard
lard
yard
shard

-are
/air/
bare
care
dare
fare
hare
mare
pare
rare
ware
blare
flare
glare
scare
share
snare
spare
square
stare

-arge
/ar/
barge
large
charge

-ark
/ar/
bark
dark
hark
lark
mark
park
Clark
shark
spark
stark

-arm
/ar/
farm
harm
charm

-arn
/ar/
barn
darn
yarn

-arp
/ar/
carp
harp
tarp
sharp

-art
/ar/
cart
dart
mart
part
tart
chart
smart
start

-ase
/ā/
base
case
vase
chase

-ash
/a/
bash
cash
dash
gash
hash
lash
mash
rash
sash
brash
clash
flash
slash
smash

stash
thrash
trash

-ask
/a/
ask
cask
mask
task
flask

-asm
/a/
chasm
spasm

-asp
/a/
gasp
hasp
rasp
clasp
grasp

-ast
/a/
cast
fast
last
mast
past
vast
blast

-aste
/ā/
baste
haste
paste
taste
waste
chaste

-ass /a/	-ate /ā/	-ave /ā/	pawn yawn brawn drawn prawn spawn	-aze /ā/	-ead /ē/	-eam /ē/	-ear /e/
bass	date	cave		daze	bead	beam	bear
lass	fate	Dave		faze	lead	ream	pear
mass	gate	gave		gaze	read	seam	wear
pass	hate	pave		haze	knead	cream	swear
brass	Kate	rave		maze	plead	dream	
class	late	save		raze		gleam	-east /ē/
glass	mate	wave		blaze	-eak /ē/	scream	
grass	rate	brave	-ax /a/	craze		steam	beast
	crate	crave		glaze	beak	stream	feast
-at /a/	grate	grave	lax	graze	leak	team	least
	plate	shave	Max		peak		yeast
bat	skate	slave	tax	-ea /ē/	teak	-ean /ē/	
cat	state	stave	wax		weak		-eat /ē/
fat			flax	pea	bleak	bean	
gnat	-ath /a/	-aw /aw/		sea	creak	dean	beat
hat			-ay /ā/	tea	freak	Jean	feat
mat	bath	caw		flea	sneak	lean	heat
pat	lath	gnaw	bay	plea	speak	mean	meat
rat	math	jaw	day		squeak	wean	neat
sat	path	law	gay	-each /ē/	streak	clean	peat
tat	wrath	paw	hay		tweak	glean	seat
vat		raw	jay	beach			bleat
brat	-aught /aw/	saw	lay	leach	-eal /ē/	-eap /ē/	cheat
chat		claw	may	peach			cleat
drat	caught	draw	nay	reach	deal	heap	pleat
flat	naught	flaw	pay	teach	heal	leap	treat
scat	taught	slaw	quay	bleach	meal	reap	wheat
slat	fraught	squaw	ray	breach	peal	cheap	
spat		straw	say	preach	real		-eave /ē/
that	-aunch /aw/		way	screech	seal	-ear /ē/	
		-awl /aw/	bray		teal		heave
-atch /a/	haunch		clay	-ead /e/	veal	dear	leave
	launch	bawl	cray		zeal	fear	weave
batch	paunch	brawl	fray	dead	squeal	gear	cleave
catch		crawl	gray	head	steal	hear	sheave
hatch	-aunt /aw/	drawl	play	lead		near	
latch		shawl	pray	read	-ealth /e/	rear	-eck /e/
match	daunt	scrawl	slay	bread		sear	
patch	gaunt	trawl	spray	dread	health	tear	deck
scratch	haunt		stay	spread	wealth	year	heck
thatch	jaunt	-awn /aw/	stray	thread	stealth	clear	neck
	taunt		sway	tread		shear	peck
	flaunt	dawn	tray			smear	check
		fawn				spear	fleck
		lawn					speck
							wreck

-ed /e/	-eed /ē/	-eem /ē/	-eet /ē/	-eld /e/	-em /e/	rend	-erge /er/
bed	deed	deem	beet	held	gem	send	merge
fed	feed	seem	feet	meld	hem	tend	serge
led	heed	teem	meet	weld	stem	vend	verge
Ned	kneed		fleet		them	wend	
red	need	-een /ē/	greet	-ell /e/		blend	-erk /er/
Ted	reed	keen	sheet	bell	-en /e/	spend	jerk
wed	seed	queen	skeet	cell	Ben	trend	clerk
bred	weed	seen	sleet	dell	den		
fled	bleed	teen	street	fell	hen	-ense /e/	-erm /er/
Fred	breed	green	sweet	hell	Ken	dense	berm
shed	creed	preen	tweet	jell	men	sense	germ
shred	freed	screen		knell	pen	tense	term
sled	greed	sheen	-eeze /ē/	Nell	ten		sperm
sped	speed		breeze	sell	yen	-ent /e/	
	steed	-eep /ē/	freeze	tell	glen	bent	-ern /er/
-edge /e/	treed	beep	sneeze	well	then	cent	fern
hedge	tweed	deep	squeeze	yell	when	dent	tern
ledge		Jeep	tweeze	dwell	wren	gent	stern
wedge	-eek /ē/	keep	wheeze	quell		Kent	
dredge	leek	peep		shell	-ence /e/	lent	-erve /er/
pledge	meek	seep	-eft /e/	smell	fence	rent	nerve
sledge	peek	weep	deft	spell	hence	sent	serve
	reek	cheep	heft	swell	whence	tent	verve
-ee /ē/	seek	creep	left			vent	swerve
bee	week	sheep	cleft	-elp /e/	-ench /e/	went	
fee	cheek	sleep	theft	help	bench	scent	-esh /e/
knee	creek	steep		kelp	wench	spent	mesh
lee	Greek	sweep	-eg /e/	yelp	clench		flesh
see	sleek		beg		drench	-ep /e/	fresh
tee		-eer /ē/	keg	-elt /e/	French	pep	
wee	-eel /ē/	beer	leg	belt	quench	rep	-ess /e/
flee	feel	deer	Meg	felt	stench	prep	Bess
free	heel	jeer	peg	knelt	trench	step	guess
glee	keel	leer		melt	wrench		less
tree	peel	peer	-eigh /ā/	pelt		-ept /e/	mess
	reel	queer	neigh	welt	-end /e/	kept	bless
-eech /ē/	creel	seer	weigh	dwelt	bend	wept	chess
beech	steel	sneer	sleigh	smelt	end	crept	dress
leech	wheel	steer			fend	slept	press
breech					lend	swept	
screech					mend		
speech							

stress	-ew	-ice	mid	grief	sniff	tight	-ill
tress	/oo/	/ī/	quid	thief	whiff	blight	/i/
	dew	dice	rid			bright	bill
-est	few	lice	grid	-ield	-ift	flight	dill
/e/	hew	mice	skid	/ē/	/i/	fright	fill
best	Jew	nice	slid	field	gift	plight	gill
guest	knew	rice		yield	lift	slight	hill
jest	new	vice	-ide	shield	rift		ill
lest	pew	price	/ī/		sift	-ike	Jill
nest	blew	slice	bide	-ier	drift	/ī/	kill
pest	brew	splice	hide	/ī/	shift	bike	mill
rest	chew	thrice	ride	brier	swift	dike	pill
test		twice	side	crier	thrift	hike	quill
vest	-ex		tide	drier		like	rill
west	/e/	-ick	wide	flier	-ig	Mike	sill
zest	hex	/i/	bride		/i/	pike	till
blest	sex	Dick	chide	-ies	big	spike	will
chest	vex	hick	glide	/ī/	dig	strike	chill
crest	flex	kick	pride	dies	fig		drill
quest		lick	slide	lies	gig	-ild	frill
wrest	-ey	Nick	snide	pies	jig	/ī/	grill
	/ā/	pick	stride	ties	pig	mild	skill
-et	hey	quick		cries	rig	wild	spill
/e/	grey	Rick	-ie	dries	wig	child	still
bet	prey	sick	/ī/	flies	brig		swill
get	they	tick	die	fries	sprig	-ile	thrill
jet	whey	wick	fie	skies	swig	/ī/	trill
let		brick	lie	tries	twig	bile	twill
met	-ib	chick	pie			file	
net	/i/	click	tie	-ife	-igh	mile	-ilt
pet	bib	flick	vie	/ī/	/ī/	Nile	/i/
set	fib	slick		fife	high	pile	gilt
wet	jib	stick	-ied	knife	nigh	tile	jilt
yet	rib	thick	/ī/	life	sigh	vile	hilt
Chet	crib	trick	died	rife	thigh	smile	kilt
fret	glib		lied	wife		stile	tilt
whet		-id	dried	strife	-ight	while	wilt
	-ibe	/i/	fried		/ī/		
-etch	/ī/	bid	tried	-iff	knight	-ilk	
/e/	jibe	did		/i/	light	/i/	
fetch	bribe	hid	-ief	miff	might	bilk	
retch	scribe	kid	/ē/	tiff	night	milk	
sketch	tribe	lid	brief	cliff	right	silk	
wretch			chief	skiff	sight		

159

			-ink	flip	-irt	bliss	site
quilt	gin	mine	/i/	grip	/er/	Swiss	white
stilt	kin	nine	kink	ship	dirt		write
	pin	pine	link	skip	flirt	-ist	sprite
-im	sin	tine	mink	slip	shirt	/i/	
/i/	tin	vine	pink	snip	skirt	fist	-ive
dim	win	wine	rink	strip	squirt	list	/ī/
him	chin	brine	sink	trip		mist	dive
Jim	grin	shine	wink	whip	-irth	wrist	five
Kim	shin	shrine	blink		/er/	grist	hive
rim	skin	spine	brink	-ipe	birth	twist	jive
Tim	spin	swine	chink	/ī/	firth		live
vim	thin	whine	clink	pipe	girth	-it	chive
brim	twin		drink	ripe	mirth	/i/	drive
grim		-ing	shrink	wipe		bit	strive
prim	-ince	/i/	slink	gripe	-ise	fit	thrive
slim	/i/	bing	stink	snipe	/ī/	hit	
swim	mince	ding	think	stripe	guise	kit	-ix
trim	since	king		swipe	rise	knit	/i/
whim	wince	ping	-int	tripe	wise	lit	fix
	prince	ring	/i/			pit	mix
-ime		sing	hint	-ir	-ish	quit	six
/ī/	-inch	wing	lint	/er/	/i/	sit	
dime	/i/	zing	mint	fir	dish	wit	-o
lime	cinch	bring	tint	sir	fish	flit	/oo/
mime	finch	cling	glint	stir	wish	grit	do
time	pinch	fling	print	whir	swish	skit	to
chime	winch	sling	splint			slit	who
clime	clinch	spring	sprint	-ird	-isk	spit	
crime	flinch	sting	squint	/er/	/i/	split	-o
grime		string	stint	bird	disk	twit	/ō/
prime	-ind	swing		gird	risk		go
slime	/ī/	thing	-ip	third	brisk	-itch	no
	bind	wring	/i/		frisk	/i/	so
-imp	find		dip	-ire	whisk	ditch	pro
/i/	hind	-inge	hip	/ī/		hitch	
limp	kind	/i/	lip	fire	-isp	pitch	-oach
chimp	mind	binge	nip	hire	/i/	witch	/ō/
crimp	rind	hinge	quip	tire	lisp	switch	coach
primp	wind	singe	rip	wire	wisp		poach
skimp	blind	tinge	sip	spire	crisp	-ite	roach
blimp	grind	cringe	tip			/ī/	broach
		fringe	zip	-irk	-iss	bite	
-in	-ine	twinge	blip	/er/	/i/	kite	-oad
/i/	/ī/		chip	quirk	hiss	mite	/ō/
bin	dine		clip	shirk	kiss	quite	goad
din	fine		drip	smirk	miss	rite	load
fin	line						

road	moat	**-od**	grog	**-old**	**-om**	lone	**-ood**
toad	gloat	/o/	slog	/ō/	/o/	tone	/ōō/
	float	cod	smog	bold	Mom	zone	food
-oak	throat	God		cold	Tom	clone	mood
/ō/		mod	**-ogue**	fold	prom	crone	brood
soak	**-ob**	nod	/ō/	gold		drone	
cloak	/o/	pod	brogue	hold	**-ome**	phone	**-oof**
croak	Bob	rod	rogue	mold	/ō/	prone	/ōō/
	cob	sod	vogue	old	dome	shone	goof
-oal	fob	Tod		sold	home	stone	roof
/ō/	gob	clod	**-oil**	told	Nome		proof
coal	job	plod	/oi/	scold	Rome	**-ong**	spoof
foal	knob	prod	boil		tome	/aw/	
goal	lob	shod	coil	**-ole**	gnome	bong	**-ook**
shoal	mob	trod	foil	/ō/	chrome	dong	/ōō/
	rob		soil	dole		gong	book
-oam	sob	**-ode**	toil	hole	**-ome**	long	cook
/ō/	blob	/ō/	spoil	mole	/u/	song	hook
foam	glob	code	broil	pole	come	tong	look
loam	slob	lode		role	some	prong	nook
roam	snob	mode	**-oin**	stole		strong	took
		node	/ol/	whole	**-omp**	thong	brook
-oan	**-obe**	rode	coin		/o/	wrong	crook
/ō/	/ō/	strode	join	**-oll**	pomp		shook
Joan	lobe		loin	/ō/	romp		
loan	robe	**-oe**	groin	poll	chomp	**-ool**	**-ool**
moan	globe	/ō/		roll	stomp	/ōō/	/ōō/
groan	probe	doe	**-oist**	toll			cool
		foe	/oi/	droll	**-on**	**-oo**	fool
-oar	**-ock**	hoe	foist	knoll	/u/	/ōō/	pool
/or/	/o/	Joe	hoist	scroll	son	boo	tool
boar	dock	toe	joist	stroll	ton	coo	drool
roar	hock	woe	moist	troll	won	goo	school
soar	knock					moo	spool
	lock	**-og**	**-oke**	**-oll**	**-ond**	poo	stool
-oast	mock	/o/	/ō/	/o/	/o/	too	
/ō/	rock	bog	coke	doll	bond	woo	**-oom**
boast	sock	cog	joke	loll	fond	zoo	/ōō/
coast	tock	dog	poke	moll	pond	shoo	boom
roast	block	fog	woke		blond		doom
toast	clock	hog	yoke	**-olt**	frond	**-ood**	loom
	crock	jog	broke	/ō/		/ōō/	room
-oat	flock	log	choke	bolt	**-one**	good	zoom
/ō/	frock	tog	smoke	colt	/ō/	hood	bloom
boat	shock	clog	spoke	jolt	bone	wood	broom
coat	smock	flog	stoke	molt	cone	stood	gloom
goat	stock	frog	stroke	volt	hone		groom

-oon
/ōō/
coon
loon
moon
noon
soon
croon
spoon
swoon

-oop
/ōō/
coop
hoop
loop
droop
scoop
sloop
snoop
stoop
swoop
troop

-oor
/or/
poor
boor
moor
spoor

-oose
/ōō/
goose
loose
moose
noose

-oot
/ōō/
boot
hoot
loot
moot
root
toot

scoot
shoot

-op
/o/
bop
cop
hop
mop
pop
sop
top
chop
crop
drop
flop
plop
prop
shop
slop
stop

-ope
/ō/
cope
dope
hope
lope
mope
nope
pope
rope
grope
scope
slope

-orch
/or/
porch
torch
scorch

-ord
/or/
cord
ford
lord

chord
sword

-ore
/or/
bore
core
fore
gore
more
pore
sore
tore
wore
chore
score
shore
snore
spore
store
swore

-ork
/or/
cork
fork
pork
York
stork

-orm
/or/
dorm
form
norm
storm

-orn
/or/
born
com
horn
mom
tom
worn
scorn
shorn

sworn
thorn

-ort
/or/
fort
Mort
port
sort
short
snort
sport

-ose
/ō/
hose
nose
pose
rose
chose
close
prose
those

-oss
/aw/
boss
loss
moss
toss
cross
floss
gloss

-ost
/aw/
cost
lost
frost

-ost
/ō/
host
most

post
ghost

-ot
/o/
cot
dot
got
hot
jot
knot
lot
not
pot
rot
tot
blot
clot
plot
shot
slot
spot
trot

-otch
/o/
botch
notch
blotch
crotch
Scotch

-ote
/ō/
note
quote
rote
vote
wrote

-oth
/aw/
moth
broth
cloth
froth
sloth

-ouch
/ow/
couch
pouch
vouch
crouch
grouch
slouch

-oud
/ow/
loud
cloud
proud

-ough
/u/
rough
slough

-ought
/aw/
bought
fought
ought
sought
brought
thought

-ould
/oo/
could
would
should

-ounce
/ow/
bounce
pounce
flounce
trounce

-ound
/ow/
bound
found
hound

mound
pound
round
sound
wound
ground

-oup
/ōō/
soup
croup
group
stoup

-our
/ow/
hour
sour
flour
scour

-ouse
/ow/
douse
house
louse
mouse
rouse
souse
blouse
grouse
spouse

-out
/ow/
bout
gout
lout
pout
rout
tout
clout
flout
grout
scout
shout
snout

spout
sprout
stout
trout

-outh
/ow/
mouth
south

-ove
/ō/
cove
wove
clove
drove
grove
stove
trove

-ove
/u/
dove
love
glove
shove

-ow
/ō/
bow
know
low
mow
row
sow
tow
blow
crow
flow
glow
grow
show
slow
snow
stow

-ow	-owse	-uck	-ue	-uke	plum	run	drunk
/ow/	/ow/	/u/	/ōō/	/ōō/	scum	sun	flunk
bow	dowse	buck	cue	duke	slum	shun	plunk
cow	browse	duck	due	nuke	strum	spun	shrunk
how	drowse	luck	hue	puke	swum	stun	skunk
now		muck	Sue	fluke			slunk
row	-ox	puck	blue		-umb	-unch	spunk
sow	/o/	suck	clue	-ule	/u/	/u/	stunk
vow	box	tuck	flue	/ū/	dumb	bunch	trunk
brow	fox	Chuck	glue	mule	numb	hunch	
chow	lox	cluck	true	pule	crumb	lunch	-unt
plow	pox	pluck		rule	plumb	munch	/u/
prow		shuck	-uff	Yule	thumb	punch	bunt
scow	-oy	stuck	/u/			brunch	hunt
	/oi/	struck	buff	-ulk	-ume	crunch	punt
-owl	boy	truck	cuff	/u/	/ōō/		runt
/ow/	coy		huff	bulk	fume	-une	blunt
fowl	joy	-ud	muff	hulk	flume	/ū/	grunt
howl	Roy	/u/	puff	sulk	plume	June	shunt
jowl	soy	bud	ruff		spume	tune	stunt
growl	toy	cud	bluff	-ull		prune	
prowl	ploy	dud	fluff	/u/	-ump		-up
scowl		mud	gruff	cull	/u/	-ung	/u/
	-ub	spud	scuff	dull	bump	/u/	cup
-own	/u/	stud	sluff	gull	dump	dung	pup
/ow/	cub	thud	snuff	hull	hump	hung	sup
down	dub		stuff	lull	jump	lung	
gown	hub	-ude		mull	lump	rung	-ur
town	nub	/ōō/	-ug	skull	pump	sung	/er/
brown	pub	dude	/u/		rump	clung	cur
clown	rub	nude	bug	-ull	chump	flung	fur
crown	sub	rude	dug	/ōō/	clump	sprung	blur
drown	tub	crude	hug	bull	frump	stung	slur
frown	club	prude	jug	full	grump	strung	spur
	drub		lug	pull	plump	swung	
	flub	-udge	mug		slump	wrung	-ure
-own	grub	/u/	pug	-um	stump		/ū/
/ō/	scrub	budge	rug	/u/	thump	-unk	cure
known	shrub	fudge	tug	bum	trump	/u/	lure
mown	snub	judge	chug	gum		bunk	pure
sown	stub	nudge	drug	hum	-un	dunk	sure
blown		drudge	plug	mum	/u/	funk	
flown	-ube	grudge	shrug	rum	bun	hunk	-url
grown	/ōō/	sludge	slug	sum	fun	junk	/er/
shown	cube	smudge	smug	chum	gun	punk	burl
thrown	rube	trudge	snug	drum	nun	sunk	curl
	tube		thug	glum	pun	chunk	furl

hurl	-urt	-use	-uss	-ut	-ute	-y	-ye
purl	/er/	/ū/	/u/	/u/	/ū/	/ī/	/ī/
churl	curt	fuse	buss	but	cute	by	aye
knurl	hurt	muse	cuss	cut	jute	my	dye
	blurt	ruse	fuss	gut	lute	cry	eye
-urn	spurt		muss	hut	mute	dry	lye
/er/		-ush	truss	jut	brute	fly	rye
burn	-us	/u/		nut	chute	fry	
turn	/u/	gush	-ust	rut	flute	ply	
churn	bus	hush	/u/	Tut		pry	
spurn	pus	lush	bust	glut	-utt	shy	
	plus	mush	dust	shut	/u/	sky	
-urse	thus	rush	gust	smut	butt	sly	
/er/		blush	just	strut	mutt	spy	
curse		brush	lust		putt	spry	
nurse		crush	must	-utch		try	
purse		flush	rust	/u/		why	
		plush	crust	Dutch			
		slush	thrust	hutch			
		thrush	trust	clutch			
				crutch			

Sight Words

These are the most common words in English, ranked in frequency order. The first 25 make up about a third of all printed material. The first 100 make up about half of all written material, and the first 300 make up about 65% of all written material. Is it any wonder that all students must learn to recognize these words instantly and to spell them correctly also? Being able to recognize these words on sight contributes significantly to reading fluency. Adding inflectional endings and common suffixes is an easy way to enlarge students' sight vocabulary.

Words 1–25	Words 26–50	Words 51–75	Words 76–100	Words 101–125	Words 125–150
the	or	will	number	over	say
of	one	up	no	new	great
and	had	other	way	sound	where
a	by	about	could	take	help
to	word	out	people	only	through
in	but	many	my	little	much
is	not	then	than	work	before
you	what	them	first	know	line
that	all	these	water	place	right
it	were	so	been	year	too
he	we	some	call	live	mean
was	when	her	who	me	old
for	your	would	oil	back	any
on	can	make	its	give	same
are	said	like	now	most	tell
as	there	him	find	very	boy
with	use	into	long	after	follow
his	an	time	down	thing	came
they	each	has	day	our	want
I	which	look	did	just	show
at	she	two	get	name	also
be	do	more	come	good	around
this	how	write	made	sentence	form
have	their	go	may	man	three
from	if	see	part	think	small

Common suffixes: *-s, -ing, -ed, -er, -ly, -est*

Words 151–175	Words 176–200	Words 201–225	Words 226–250	Words 251–275	Words 276–300
set	try	high	saw	important	miss
put	kind	every	left	until	idea
end	hand	near	don't	children	enough
does	picture	add	few	side	eat
another	again	food	while	feet	facet
well	change	between	along	car	watch
large	off	own	might	mile	far
must	play	below	close	night	Indian
big	spell	country	something	walk	really
even	air	plant	seem	white	almost
such	away	last	next	sea	let
because	animal	school	hard	began	above
turn	house	father	open	grow	girl
here	point	keep	example	took	sometimes
why	page	tree	begin	river	mountain
ask	letter	never	life	four	cut
went	mother	start	always	carry	young
men	answer	city	those	state	talk
read	found	earth	both	once	soon
need	study	eye	paper	book	list
land	still	light	together	hear	song
different	learn	thought	got	stop	being
home	should	head	group	without	leave
us	America	under	often	second	family
move	world	story	run	later	it's

Common suffixes: *-s, -ing, -ed, -er, -ly, -est*

Words 301–320	Words 341–360	Words 381–400	Words 421–440	Words 461–480	Words 501–520
body	hours	cold	front	warm	can't
music	black	cried	feel	common	matter
color	products	plan	fact	bring	square
stand	happened	notice	inches	explain	syllables
sun	whole	south	street	dry	perhaps
question	measure	sing	decided	though	bill
fish	remember	war	contain	language	felt
area	early	ground	course	shape	suddenly
mark	waves	fall	surface	deep	test
dog	reached	king	produce	thousands	direction
horse	listen	town	building	yes	center
birds	wind	I'll	ocean	clear	farmers
problem	rock	unit	class	equation	ready
complete	space	figure	note	yet	anything
room	covered	certain	nothing	government	divided
knew	fast	field	rest	filled	general
since	several	travel	carefully	heat	energy
ever	hold	wood	scientists	full	subject
piece	himself	fire	inside	hot	Europe
told	toward	upon	wheels	check	moon

Words 321–340	Words 361–380	Words 401–420	Words 441–460	Words 481–500	Words 521–540
usually	five	done	stay	object	region
didn't	step	English	green	bread	return
friends	morning	road	known	rule	believe
easy	passed	halt	island	among	dance
heard	vowel	ten	week	noun	members
order	true	fly	less	power	picked
red	hundred	gave	machine	cannot	simple
door	against	box	base	able	cells
sure	pattern	finally	ago	six	paint
become	numeral	wait	stood	size	mind
top	table	correct	plane	dark	love
ship	north	oh	system	ball	cause
across	slowly	quickly	behind	material	rain
today	money	person	ran	special	exercise
during	map	became	round	heavy	eggs
short	farm	shown	boat	fine	train
better	pulled	minutes	game	pair	blue
best	draw	strong	force	circle	wish
however	voice	verb	brought	include	drop
low	seen	stars	understand	built	developed

Words 541–560	Words 581–600	Words 621–640	Words 661–680	Words 701–720	Words 741–760
window	west	buy	possible	row	east
difference	lay	century	gold	least	pay
distance	weather	outside	milk	catch	single
heart	root	everything	quiet	climbed	touch
sit	instruments	tall	natural	wrote	information
sum	meet	already	lot	shouted	express
summer	third	instead	stone	continued	mouth
wall	months	phrase	act	itself	yard
forest	paragraph	soil	build	else	equal
probably	raised	bed	middle	plains	decimal
legs	represent	copy	speed	gas	yourself
sat	soft	free	count	England	control
main	whether	hope	cat	burning	practice
winter	clothes	spring	someone	design	report
wide	flowers	case	sail	joined	straight
written	shall	laughed	rolled	foot	rise
length	teacher	nation	bear	law	statement
reason	held	quite	wonder	ears	stick
kept	describe	type	smiled	grass	party
interest	drive	themselves	angle	you're	seeds

Words 561–580	Words 601–620	Words 641–660	Words 681–700	Words 721–740	Words 761–780
arms	cross	temperature	fraction	grew	suppose
brother	speak	bright	Africa	skin	woman
race	solve	lead	killed	valley	coast
present	appear	everyone	melody	cents	bank
beautiful	metal	method	bottom	key	period
store	son	section	trip	president	wire
job	either	lake	hole	brown	choose
edge	ice	consonant	poor	trouble	clean
past	sleep	within	let's	cool	visit
sign	village	dictionary	fight	cloud	bit
record	factors	hair	surprise	lost	whose
finished	result	age	French	sent	received
discovered	jumped	amount	died	symbols	garden
wild	snow	scale	beat	wear	please
happy	ride	pounds	exactly	bad	strange
beside	care	although	remain	save	caught
gone	floor	per	dress	experiment	fell
sky	hill	broken	iron	engine	team
glass	pushed	moment	couldn't	alone	God
million	baby	tiny	fingers	drawing	captain

Words 781–800	Words 821–840	Words 861–880	Words 901–920	Words 941–960	Words 981–1,000
direct	fit	position	company	shoes	rope
ring	addition	entered	radio	actually	cotton
serve	belong	fruit	we'll	nose	apple
child	safe	tied	action	afraid	details
desert	soldiers	rich	capital	dead	entire
increase	guess	dollars	factories	sugar	corn
history	silent	send	settled	adjective	substances
cost	trade	sight	yellow	fig	smell
maybe	rather	chief	isn't	office	tools
business	compare	Japanese	southern	huge	conditions
separate	crowd	stream	truck	gun	cows
break	poem	planets	fair	similar	track
uncle	enjoy	rhythm	printed	death	arrived
hunting	elements	eight	wouldn't	score	located
flow	indicate	science	ahead	forward	sir
lady	except	major	chance	stretched	seat
students	expect	observe	born	experience	division
human	flat	tube	level	rose	effect
art	seven	necessary	triangle	allow	underline
feeling	interesting	weight	molecules	fear	view

Words 801–820	Words 841–860	Words 881–900	Words 921–940	Words 961–980
supply	sense	meat	France	workers
corner	string	lifted	repeated	Washington
electric	blow	process	column	Greek
insects	famous	army	western	women
crops	value	hat	church	bought
tone	wings	property	sister	led
hit	movement	particular	oxygen	march
sand	pole	swim	plural	northern
doctor	exciting	terms	various	create
provide	branches	current	agreed	British
thus	thick	park	opposite	difficult
won't	blood	sell	wrong	match
cook	lie	shoulder	chart	win
bones	spot	industry	prepared	doesn't
tail	bell	wash	pretty	steel
board	fun	block	solution	total
modern	loud	spread	fresh	deal
compound	consider	cattle	shop	determine
mine	suggested	wife	suffix	evening
wasn't	thin	sharp	especially	nor

Index

Note. *f* following a page number indicates a figure.

Academic achievement. *See also* Reading difficulties in general
  emotional factors, 22–23
  exercise and, 21
  nutrition and, 13
  sleep and, 19
Activating prior knowledge strategies, 123–124. *See also* Comprehension
Activities to do with your child to address difficulties. *See also* Difficulties, identification of; Games; Resources to help you address your child's difficulties
  ability to manipulate sounds within words, 83–85
  ability to perceive and generate beginning, ending, and medial sounds, 79–82
  ability to perceive and generate rhymes, 78–79
  ability to perceive words within sentences, 76–78
  auditory processing difficulties, 74–85
  beginning consonant difficulties, 92–95
  comprehension difficulties, 122–130
  consonant blends difficulties, 99–101
  creating an environment that helps with focus, 136–137
  determining and monitoring reading levels, 134–135
  digraph difficulties, 101–102
  diphthong difficulties, 102–103
  ending consonant difficulties, 95–96
  guided reading lessons, 129–130
  helping readers realize they aren't understanding what they're reading, 126–127
  at-home environment that supports vocabulary, 110–111
  learning specific vocabulary for texts, 111–115, 113*f*, 114*f*
  letter recognition and, 61–65
  long-vowel difficulties, 98–99
  oral language techniques, 107–108
  phonics skills, 92–103
  short-vowel difficulties, 96–98
  sight words and, 67–69
  strategies for constructing the meaning of a text, 123–124
  strategies for monitoring if readers are comprehending the text, 124–126
  strengthening attention, 137–138
  strengthening motivation, 139–143
  teaching comprehension strategies, 128–129
  thematic learning activities, 108–109
  visual processing difficulties, 61–69
  vocabulary, 107–115
  word families/phonograms and, 65–67
  word study, 110
Adult–child relationships, 23–25, 141
Advocating for your child, 55–56. *See also* Professional help
Ask for help strategy, 127. *See also* Comprehension
Attention. *See also* Motivation; Parallel distributed processing model (PDPM); Text difficulty
  activities for strengthening, 137–138
  Attention Checklist, 36, 52
  creating an environment that helps with focus, 136–137
  identifying difficulty in, 52

Attention (continued)
limited internal attention and, 35–36
Motivation Checklist, 36
overview, 10, 26, 30f, 37–38, 132–133, 135–136
Auditory processing. See also Phonological processor; Speech
ability to manipulate sounds within words, 83–85
ability to perceive and generate beginning, ending, and medial sounds, 79–82
ability to perceive and generate rhymes, 78–79
ability to perceive words within sentences, 76–78
addressing difficulties with, 74–85
Auditory Processing Checklist, 32, 45–47, 72
identifying difficulty in, 45–47
overview, 9–10, 31–32, 37–38, 72–73, 85–86
phonics and, 47
relationship of to reading, 73
Avoidant behaviors, 26. See also Behavior

Background knowledge, 123–124
Bedtime routine, 20. See also Sleep
Beginning sounds. See also Sound processing
ability to manipulate sounds within words, 83, 84
addressing difficulties with, 80, 86
Behavior. See also Brain functioning; Foundations of reading
Behavioral Checklist, 43
emotional factors and, 23, 26
identifying difficulty in, 43
improving, 27–28
literacy pyramid and, 13f
overview, 9, 26–28
Book levels. See Reading levels; Text difficulty
Books. See also Resources to help you address your child's difficulties
beginning consonant difficulties, 93–95
consonant blends difficulties, 100
digraph difficulties, 101
diphthongs difficulties, 102–103
ending consonant difficulties, 96
letter recognition and, 62–63
long-vowel difficulties, 99
selection of to increase motivation, 139–140
short-vowel difficulties, 97
word families/phonograms and, 66

Brain functioning. See also Foundations of reading
connectionism and, 35
emotional factors, 22–23
exercise and, 21
nutrition and, 13, 14
overview, 9–10
sleep and, 19
visual processing and, 59–60

Cause–effect type of informational text, 121
Character in narrative text, 119
Checklists
Attention Checklist, 36, 52
Auditory Processing Checklist, 32, 45–47, 72
Behavioral Checklist, 43
Comprehension and Metacognition Checklist, 35, 49–50
Emotional Well-Being Checklist, 42–43
Exercise Checklist, 41–42
Motivation Checklist, 36, 53
Nutrition Checklist, 40–42
overview, 10
Phonics Skills Checklist, 32, 47–48, 88
Sleep Checklist, 41
Visual Processing Checklist, 31, 44–45, 47, 58
Vocabulary Skills Checklist, 34, 48–49
Choice, 140, 141
Close reading, 119–120
Cognitive functioning, 22–23
Collaboration, 140
Communication with your child, 23–25, 141
Comparison—contrast type of informational text, 121
Compound words, 83. See also Word sounds
Comprehension. See also Context processor; Metacognition
addressing difficulties with, 122–130
Comprehension and Metacognition Checklist, 35, 49–50
determining and monitoring reading levels and, 134
guided reading lessons, 129–130
helping readers realize they aren't understanding what they're reading, 126–127
identifying difficulty in, 49–50
limited internal attention and, 35–36
overview, 10, 34–35, 37–38, 117–118, 130
parallel distributed processing model (PDPM) and, 5–6, 6f

strategies for constructing the meaning of a text, 123–124
strategies for monitoring if readers are comprehending the text, 124–126
teaching comprehension strategies, 128–129
text structure and, 118–122
Comprehension fix-up strategies. *See* Comprehension; Fix-up strategies
Connectionism, 35, 37–38, 59–60
Consonant blends, 91, 99–101. *See also* Consonants; Phonics
Consonants. *See also* Letter sounds; Phonics
addressing beginning consonant difficulties, 92–95
addressing difficulties with consonant blends, 91, 99–101
addressing difficulties with digraphs, 101–102
addressing ending consonant difficulties, 95–96
overview, 91
Content knowledge, 13*f*, 147–149, 150–151. *See also* Thematic learning
Context processor, 5–6, 6*f*, 29–30, 30*f*, 34–35, 37–38. *See also* Comprehension; Parallel distributed processing model (PDPM)
Corrections, 141

Diagnosis, 7, 36, 37–38
Diet. *See* Nutrition
Difficulties, identification of. *See also* Activities to do with your child to address difficulties; Checklists
advocating for your child and, 55–56
attention, 52
auditory processing, 45–47
behavior, 43
comprehension, 49–50
difficulties in more than one area, 53
emotional well-being, 42–43
exercise, 40–42
metacognition, 49–50
motivation, 52–53
nutrition, 40–42
overview, 10, 39–40, 54
parallel distributed processing model (PDPM) and, 37
phonics, 47–48
physiological factors, 40–42
sleep, 40–42
visual processing, 44–45
vocabulary, 48–49
when to seek professional help, 53–54

Difficulty of text. *See* Text difficulty
Digraphs, 92, 101–102. *See also* Phonics
Diphthongs, 92, 102–103. *See also* Phonics
Distractions. *See* Attention; Environmental distractions
Dyslexia, 7. *See also* Reading difficulties in general

Electronics and screens, use of, 20, 148
Emotional well-being. *See also* Brain functioning; Feelings; Foundations of reading
Emotional Well-Being Checklist, 42–43
identifying difficulty in, 42–43
literacy pyramid and, 13*f*
overview, 9, 22–26
Ending sounds. *See also* Sound processing
ability to manipulate sounds within words, 83, 84–85
addressing difficulties with, 80–81, 86
Enumeration—description type of informational text, 121
Environmental distractions. *See also* Attention
creating an environment that helps with focus, 136–137
at-home environment that supports vocabulary, 110–111
overview, 135–136
Evaluation, professional, 53–54, 55–56
Exercise, 9, 21–22, 40–42. *See also* Brain functioning; Foundations of reading; Physiological factors
Explanation—process type of informational text, 121
Extrinsic motivation, 139. *See also* Motivation
Eye examination, 61, 70

Famous people who have struggled with reading, 10–11
Feelings. *See* Emotional well-being
behaviors associated with, 23, 26
communicating with your child regarding, 23–25
helping your child to manage, 25–26
Fix-up strategies, 34–35, 126–127. *See also* Comprehension
Focus, 26. *See also* Attention
Food. *See* Nutrition
Foundations of reading, 9, 12, 13*f*. *See also* Behavior; Brain functioning; Emotional well-being; Exercise; Nutrition; Sleep

Games. *See also* Activities to do with your child to address difficulties; Resources to help you address your child's difficulties
 ability to perceive and generate rhymes, 78–79
 ability to perceive words within sentences, 76–78
 consonant blends difficulties, 100–101
 digraphs difficulties, 101
 ending consonant difficulties, 95–96
 increasing vocabulary, 111
 letter recognition and, 62
 long-vowel difficulties, 98–99
 short-vowel difficulties, 98
 sight words and, 68–69
 strengthening attention, 137–138
Goal in narrative text, 119
Guided reading, 129–130. *See also* Comprehension

Hearing, 73
Hierarchy of needs, 4–5, 5f, 12, 13f
High-frequency sight words, 67–69, 70. *See also* Sight words
Hydration, 15. *See also* Nutrition

Identification of difficulties. *See* Checklists; Difficulties, identification of
Inactivity. *See* Exercise
Informational text, 120–122, 129–130. *See also* Comprehension; Text structure
Interletter associational unit system, 30–31, 60
Internal attention. *See* Attention; Limited internal attention
Intervention, professional
 advocating for your child and, 55–56
 eye examinations and, 61
 when to seek, 53–54
Intrinsic motivation, 139. *See also* Motivation

Letter recognition. *See also* Letter sounds; Phonograms; Word families
 addressing difficulties with visual processing and, 61–65, 70
 brain processes involved in, 59
 overview, 30–31
 speed of, 61–65, 70
Letter sounds. *See also* Consonants; Letter recognition; Sound processing; Vowels; Word sounds
 beginning sounds, 80, 83, 84, 86
 ending sounds, 80–81, 83, 84–85, 86
 medial sounds, 81–82, 85, 86

Letterbox, brain's, 59–60, 65. *See also* Brain functioning
Level, reading. *See* Reading levels; Text difficulty
Limited internal attention, 35–36. *See also* Attention
Lists, word. *See* Word lists
Literacy pyramid. *See also* Foundations of reading
 behavior, 13f, 26–28
 content knowledge, 13f
 emotional factors, 13f, 22–26
 literacy skills, 13f
 overview, 12, 13f, 39–40, 147–149, 147f
 physiological foundation of, 13–22, 13f
 self-actualization, 13f
Literacy skills, 13f
Long vowels, 91, 98–99. *See also* Phonics; Vowels
Look up a word strategy, 127. *See also* Comprehension

Maslow's hierarchy of needs, 4–5, 5f, 12, 13f
Meal planning, 16. *See also* Nutrition
Meaning processor, 5–6, 6f, 29–30, 30f, 33–34, 37–38. *See also* Comprehension; Parallel distributed processing model (PDPM); Vocabulary
Medial sounds. *See also* Sound processing
 ability to manipulate sounds within words, 85
 addressing difficulties with, 81–82, 86
Metacognition. *See also* Comprehension; Context processor
 activities for helping readers realize they aren't understanding what they're reading, 126–127
 Comprehension and Metacognition Checklist, 35, 49–50
 identifying difficulty in, 49–50
 overview, 10, 34, 37–38, 117–118, 130
 strategies for monitoring if readers are comprehending the text, 124–126
Motivation. *See also* Attention; Parallel distributed processing model (PDPM); Text difficulty
 Attention Checklist, 36
 identifying difficulty in, 52–53
 limited internal attention and, 35–36
 Maslow's hierarchy of needs and, 4–5, 5f, 12, 13f
 Motivation Checklist, 36, 53
 overview, 10, 30f, 37–38, 132–133, 138–139, 143

relationship of to reading, 139
strengthening, 139–143
Multisensory materials. *See also* Resources to
    help you address your child's difficulties
beginning consonant difficulties, 93
digraph difficulties, 101
letter recognition and, 62
long-vowel difficulties, 98–99
strengthening attention, 138

Narrative text, 119–121. *See also*
    Comprehension; Text structure
Neuroscience. *See* Brain functioning
Nutrition. *See also* Brain functioning;
    Foundations of reading; Physiological
    factors
foods to avoid, 14–15
identifying difficulty in, 40–42
improving, 15–19
Nutrition Checklist, 40–41
overview, 9, 13–19
sleep and, 20

Omega-3 fatty acids, 15. *See also* Nutrition
Oppositional behaviors, 26. *See also*
    Behavior
Oral language, 107–108. *See also* Vocabulary
Orthographic processor. *See also* Parallel
    distributed processing model (PDPM);
    Print processing
low-level processors and, 32–33
overview, 29–31, 30f, 37–38
parallel distributed processing model
    (PDPM) and, 5–6, 6f
Outcome in narrative text, 119

Parallel distributed processing model
    (PDPM). *See also* Attention; Context
    processor; Meaning processor;
    Motivation; Orthographic processor;
    Phonological processor; Text difficulty
connectionism and, 35
as a diagnostic tool, 36
limited internal attention and, 35–36
low-level processors and, 32–33
overview, 5–6, 6f, 9–10, 29–30, 30f, 37–38
weaknesses in multiple processors and, 37
Phonemic awareness, 75, 79–85
Phonics. *See also* Parallel distributed
    processing model (PDPM); Print and
    sound matching; Print processing;
    Sound processing; Word sounds
addressing difficulties with, 92–103
Auditory Processing Checklist, 47

beginning consonant difficulties, 92–95
causes of difficulties in, 89–92
digraph difficulties, 101–102
diphthongs difficulties, 102–103
ending consonant difficulties, 95–96
identifying difficulty in, 47–48
long-vowel difficulties, 98–99
low-level processors and, 32–33
overview, 5–6, 6f, 9–10, 30f, 32, 37–38,
    88–89, 103
Phonics Skills Checklist, 32, 47–48, 88
relationship of to reading, 89
short-vowel difficulties, 96–98
Visual Processing Checklist, 47
Phonograms, 65–67, 70
Phonological awareness, 74–75, 76–78
Phonological processor. *See also* Auditory
    processing; Parallel distributed
    processing model (PDPM); Sound
    processing
low-level processors and, 32–33
overview, 29–30, 30f, 31–32, 37–38
parallel distributed processing model
    (PDPM) and, 5–6, 6f
Physical activity. *See* Exercise
Physiological factors. *See also* Exercise;
    Nutrition; Sleep
checklists, 40–42
identifying difficulty in, 40–42
literacy pyramid and, 13f
Maslow's hierarchy of needs and, 12,
    13f
overview, 13–22
Plant-based diet, 14–15, 16. *See also*
    Nutrition
Plot in narrative text, 119
Predicting strategy, 124. *See also*
    Comprehension
Previewing strategies, 123. *See also*
    Comprehension
Print and sound matching. *See* Phonics;
    Word sounds
Print processing. *See also* Orthographic
    processor; Parallel distributed
    processing model (PDPM); Phonics;
    Print and sound matching; Visual
    processing
overview, 5–6, 6f, 30f, 37–38
Phonics Skills Checklist, 32, 47–48
Prior knowledge, 123–124
Problem in narrative text, 119
Problem–solution type of informational
    text, 121
Process of reading. *See* Reading process

Professional help
advocating for your child, 55–56
eye examinations, 61
when to seek, 53–54

Reading comprehension. *See*
Comprehension
Reading difficulties in general. *See also*
Academic achievement; Dyslexia
example of, 148–150
limited internal attention and, 35–36
overview, 3–6, 5*f*, 6*f*, 150–151
what you've learned about, 145–146
Reading levels, 50–51, 134–135. *See also*
Text difficulty
Reading process. *See also* Parallel distributed
processing model (PDPM)
guided reading lessons and, 129–130
learning specific vocabulary for texts,
111–115, 113*f*, 114*f*
overview, 29–30
what you've learned about, 145–146
Recommendations. *See* Activities to do
with your child to address difficulties;
Resources to help you address your
child's difficulties
Reorient strategy, 126. *See also*
Comprehension
Reread strategy, 126. *See also*
Comprehension
Resources to help you address your child's
difficulties. *See also* Activities to do
with your child to address difficulties;
Books; Games; Multisensory materials;
Websites
beginning consonant difficulties, 93–95
consonant blends difficulties, 100–101
ending consonant difficulties, 95–96
letter recognition and, 62–65
long-vowel difficulties, 98–99
short-vowel difficulties, 97–98
sight words and, 68–69
strengthening attention, 137–138
word families/phonograms and, 66–69
Rewards, 27–28, 139. *See also* Behavior;
Motivation
Rhyme, 74, 78–79

Schemata, 33. *See also* Meaning processor
Self-harming behavior, 26. *See also* Behavior
Semantic maps and feature analysis charts,
113, 113*f*, 114*f*
Sentences, 76–78

Setting a purpose for reading strategy, 124.
See also Comprehension
Setting in narrative text, 119
Short vowels, 91, 96–98. *See also* Phonics;
Vowels
Sight words, 67–69, 70
Signposts when reading, 119–120
Sleep, 9, 19–21, 40–42. *See also* Brain
functioning; Foundations of reading;
Physiological factors
Sleep-dependent memory consolidation, 19
Slow down strategy, 126. *See also*
Comprehension
Snacks, 18. *See also* Nutrition
Social collaboration, 140
Songs, 77–78. *See also* Activities to do with
your child to address difficulties
Sound processing. *See also* Auditory
processing; Letter sounds; Phonics;
Phonological processor; Print and
sound matching; Speech
addressing difficulties with, 79–85
Auditory Processing Checklist, 32
overview, 31–32, 37–38
parallel distributed processing model
(PDPM) and, 5–6, 6*f*
phonics and, 32
Phonics Skills Checklist, 47–48
Speech, 5–6, 6*f*, 30*f*. *See also* Auditory
processing; Parallel distributed
processing model (PDPM); Sound
processing
Strengths, identification of, 10
Stress, 23
Summarizing strategy, 126. *See also*
Comprehension
Syllables, 83

Take a break strategy, 127. *See also*
Comprehension
Tantrums, 26. *See also* Behavior
Television, 20, 148
Text difficulty. *See also* Attention;
Motivation; Parallel distributed
processing model (PDPM); Reading
levels
determining and monitoring reading
levels, 50–51, 134–135
limited internal attention and, 35–36
overview, 10, 30*f*, 37–38, 132–135
Text structure, 118–122. *See also*
Comprehension
Thematic learning, 108–109. *See also*
Content knowledge

Thematic sight words, 69, 70. *See also* Sight words

Time sequence type of informational text, 121

Treatment, professional, 53–54, 55–56

Venn diagrams, 114–115, 114*f*

Violent behaviors, 26. *See also* Behavior

Visual processing. *See also* Print processing
addressing difficulties with, 61–65, 70
brain processes involved in, 59–60
causes of visual processing difficulty, 61
identifying difficulty in, 44–45
letter recognition and, 61–65
overview, 9–10, 30–31, 37–38, 58–59
phonics and, 47
sight words and, 67–69
Visual Processing Checklist, 31, 44–45, 58
word families/phonograms and, 65–67

Visualizing strategy, 125, 129. *See also* Comprehension

Vocabulary. *See also* Meaning processor
activities for increasing, 107–115
guided reading lessons and, 130
at-home environment that supports, 110–111
identifying difficulty in, 48–49
learning specific vocabulary for texts, 111–115, 113*f*, 114*f*
oral language techniques, 107–108
overview, 33–34, 37–38, 105–106, 115
parallel distributed processing model (PDPM) and, 5–6, 6*f*
thematic learning activities, 108–109
vocabulary development, 9–10
Vocabulary Skills Checklist, 34, 48–49
word study, 110

Vowels. *See also* Letter sounds; Phonics
diphthongs difficulties, 102–103
long-vowel difficulties, 91, 98–99
overview, 91
short-vowel difficulties, 91, 96–98

Weaknesses. *See* Difficulties, identification of

Websites. *See also* Resources to help you address your child's difficulties
addressing difficulties with consonant blends, 100–101
addressing difficulties with digraphs, 102
addressing difficulties with diphthongs, 103
addressing long-vowel difficulties, 99
determining and monitoring reading levels and, 134–135
letter recognition and, 63–64
strengthening attention, 138
strengthening motivation and, 143
word families/phonograms and, 66–67

Well-being, emotional. *See* Emotional well-being

Whole-food diet, 14–15, 16. *See also* Nutrition

Word families, 65–67, 70

Word lists, 65–66, 67–68

Word meanings, 33–34, 37–38. *See also* Meaning processor; Vocabulary

Word reading, 60

Word sounds. *See also* Letter sounds; Phonics; Print and sound matching; Sound processing
ability to manipulate, 83–85
ability to perceive and generate beginning, ending, and medial sounds, 79–82
addressing difficulties with, 86
beginning consonant difficulties, 92–95
consonant blends difficulties, 99–101
digraph difficulties, 101–102
diphthongs difficulties, 102–103
ending consonant difficulties, 95–96
long-vowel difficulties, 98–99
short-vowel difficulties, 96–98

Word study, 110–111

About the Author

Diane H. Tracey, EdD, recently retired as Professor of Education at Kean University, where she served on the faculty for 25 years. A recipient of Kean's Presidential Scholars Challenge Award, she has written widely on topics related to literacy achievement. Dr. Tracey is currently training for her second career—to become a psychoanalyst—and is working as a psychotherapist at the Center for Modern Psychoanalytic Studies in New York City. The mother of two grown children and grandmother of four, Dr. Tracey is deeply committed to helping children grow physically, emotionally, cognitively, and morally.